REVISITING JOURNEYS

Other Redleaf Press books by Miriam Beloglovsky
Just Play: Inspiring Adult Play in Early Childhood Education
Loose Parts for Children with Diverse Abilities

Coauthored by Miriam Beloglovsky and Lisa Daly
Early Learning Theories Made Visible
Loose Parts: Inspiring Play in Young Children
Loose Parts 2: Inspiring Play with Infants and Toddlers
Loose Parts 3: Inspiring Culturally Sustainable Environments
Loose Parts 4: Inspiring 21st Century Learning

Coauthored by Miriam Beloglovsky and Michelle Grant-Groves
Design in Mind: A Framework for Sparking Ideas, Collaboration, and Innovation in Early Education

REVISITING JOURNEYS

Understanding How Children Reflect, Reimagine, and Redesign Their Play and Learning

Miriam Beloglovsky and Jessica Frazier

redleafpress
A THINK SMALL BRAND

Published by Redleaf Press
10 Yorkton Court
St. Paul, MN 55117
www.redleafpress.org

First edition 2026
Cover design based on design ideas provided by Mayra Walters
Interior design by Becky Daum
Typeset in Adobe Garamond Pro
Photographs by Miriam Beloglovsky, Jessica Frazier, and Alex Dolan
Printed in the United States of America
32 31 30 29 28 27 26 25 1 2 3 4 5 6 7 8

Cataloging-in-Publication Data is on file with the Library of Congress

Printed on acid-free paper

We dedicate this book to Diego, Jessie and Alex's son, and Eliana Luis, Arielle and Max's daughter and Miriam's granddaughter. They were born as we wrote it. Their laughter and milestones fill our hearts with joy and hope for the future.

Contents

ACKNOWLEDGMENTS ix

INTRODUCTION 1

CHAPTER 1: Defining a Revisiting Journey 7

CHAPTER 2: Revisiting Play and Learning 21

CHAPTER 3: Ecosystems as the Foundations for Children's Revisiting Journeys 35

CHAPTER 4: Embarking on Educator Parallel Journeys 47

CHAPTER 5: Chronicles as Collaboration 55

CHAPTER 6: Learning Through Inductive Reasoning: A Journey into Color Theory 67

CHAPTER 7: Learning Through Scientific Thinking: A Journey into Natural Ink Making 89

CHAPTER 8: Learning Through Replication: A Journey into Spinners (Spirals) and Mandalas 105

CHAPTER 9: Learning Through Analysis and Evaluation: A Journey into the Local Ecosystem 123

CHAPTER 10: Learning Through Representation: A Journey into Identity Through Stitching Stories 141

CHAPTER 11: Learning Through Power: A Journey Through Fire into Shelter 153

CHAPTER 12: Learning Through Nature: A Journey with Birds 171

CHAPTER 13: Learning Through Story Making: A Yearlong Journey into Storytelling 191

CONCLUSION: Jessie and Miriam's Revisiting Journeys 205

REFERENCES 207

INDEX 209

Acknowledgments

This book's value comes from the excellent programs that took a risk and shared their stories of revisiting journeys. To Paola Lopez and the educators at Kinderoo Children's Academy in Ocala, Florida, your stories have been a profound source of inspiration. To Alex Morgan, Alison Maher, and the incredibly talented educators at Boulder Journey School, your shared stories have sparked creativity and innovation. To Cindy Gennarelli and Lauren Dutch from William Paterson University Child Development Center, your stories have illustrated the value of caring and trusting children. To Marissa Sumler and Taylor Mandell, your children's stories and photos have invited us to learn to see every child's brilliance. We also want to thank Michelle Grant for letting us photograph at the Center of Gravity preschool. Its beautiful design served as inspiration. To Alex Dolan for photographing and capturing the beauty in the children's work: We could not have written this book without you.

Jessie would like to thank her parents, Teri and Max Frazier, for their unwavering support and encouragement. She thanks her sister, Allison Finley, for always being a beacon of strength, and Marissa Rizo for being her most critical friend and thinking partner. Exploring children's curiosities with you, Marissa, is why I love working in early childhood education.

Miriam would like to acknowledge her critical friends and fellow advocates, Margie, Consuelo, Paulina, Michelle, Cheryl, Joya, Kathryn, Lily, and Lydia, for their ongoing support and inspiration. May we continue to advocate for change together.

Introduction

We write this book to share our observations, experiences, and research on how children approach learning. We want to dismantle the notion that learning is linear and question the premise of step-up achievement, in which children must perform and meet outcomes to be acknowledged and respected and in which the child who acts according to adult expectations is favored over the child with independent and creative ideas.

We also want to discuss how learning can be more engaging in the primary grades. Learning takes more than memorizing information, completing worksheets, doing adult-created lesson plans, reviewing calendars, or taking tests. We have found that learning halts when a routine or activity is designed to elicit compliance. For instance, requiring children to line up to go outdoors takes too long and infringes on children's outdoor time. Completing an adult-designed craft limits children's creativity and stunts their imagination. These disruptive routines and activities not only hinder learning but also create tension and distrust between educators and children. They encourage educators to focus on ensuring that children line up or perfectly construct the craft instead of encouraging more effective and safe transition routines and more creative art explorations.

We want to demonstrate that daily practices grounded in an authentic understanding of child development and in curiosity to see what children will do leads to higher growth and development. We believe that learning needs to be meaningful and joyful. Children are naturally curious and need adults to create safe and nurturing environments where their curiosity can thrive.

When educators shift from exerting power and control to encouraging revisiting journeys, children can use their experiences to broaden and solidify their learning. Revisiting journeys happen when children follow an interest and go deeper into their investigations, repeatedly revisiting, redesigning, and reflecting on what changes or additions are still needed. By watching revisiting journeys, educators will find authentic data to guide their practices. Revisiting journeys can dismantle systems of privilege, as revisiting journeys focus on designing a more equitable and inclusive ecosystem that gives space to diverse voices.

Revisiting the Organization of This Book

Life is an ongoing journey of discovery and learning. All people have unique ways of engaging with information, absorbing knowledge, and making sense of the world. This book is organized to empower you to chart your own learning path by selecting the areas you want to read first and then coming back and revisiting them as you discover new information. The process allows you to explore and learn at your own pace.

One vivid example of this individuality is how people approach reading books. Diverse approaches reflect individuals' personal curiosity that leads to their learning and understanding. Some people might read every page meticulously. Other people might flip through the pages quickly, pausing only to examine the photographs or illustrations that catch their eye. For them, these visuals serve as gateways to deeper understanding; they spark curiosity and guide subsequent reading. Still others might dive straight into the chapter that resonates most with their current interests or needs. This selective approach allows them to extract immediate value from the text, tailoring the reading experience to suit their objectives. Likewise, when children enter a revisiting journey, they follow a path that interests them. Freedom of choice in reading and learning empowers individuals to explore and discover in ways that are most meaningful and effective for them. Each approach is valid; there's no correct way to read a book, just as there is no single right way to learn.

Flexibility can help you as you navigate a book according to your preferences and interests; you can steer your learning experiences in ways that align with your strengths, goals, and curiosities. Self-directed learning is not just a choice but a pressing necessity in today's fast-paced world, where information is abundant and demands on your time and attention are ever increasing. By embracing self-directed learning, you empower yourself to pursue knowledge in ways that are most meaningful and effective for you.

Ultimately, embracing your unique learning path fosters a lifelong learning culture. When you view learning as a dynamic, individualized process, you become more open to new ideas and experiences. You develop the resilience and adaptability needed to navigate an always-changing world. You cultivate a sense of curiosity and wonder that drives you to continually seek new knowledge and skills. However you decide to read this book, we invite you to revisit it often and let your curiosity guide you.

In chapter 1, we define the revisiting journeys framework that facilitates the design, implementation, and documentation of revisiting journeys. We look at how children enter various revisiting journeys through inquiry, and we introduce the term *heutagogy*, coined by Stewart Hase and Chris Kenyon. Heutagogy is a student-centered instructional approach emphasizing self-determined learning. Learners take ownership of their learning journey and develop autonomy, capacity, and capability. Although the term applies to adult learning, we believe that it also translates into work with young children.

In chapter 2, we reimagine play and learning in a way that facilitates how children engage in revisiting. We also share research that identifies eighteen unique types of revisiting journeys. In chapter 3, we discuss in detail how to design a responsive play ecosystem to support revisiting journeys. In chapter 4, we introduce the concept of the parallel journeys of discovery and learning you take when revisiting with young children. And in chapter 5, we guide you through the process of chronicling revisiting journeys.

Chapters 6 through 13 bring revisiting journeys to life through alluring photographs and compelling stories, capturing the essences of multiple educational explorations. For instance, we remember the radiant smiles of children as they navigated through re-created scenes of historical events, fully engaged and immersed in their learning. As educators, we too found immense value in these journeys, witnessing firsthand how the revisiting journeys framework looks in practice, and how both children and educators engaged in parallel learning journeys.

Are you ready for a journey of rediscovery? You can embark on a personal revisiting journey as you delve into this book. Throughout this book, we pose a series of reflective questions to help you think about how you can use the revisiting journeys framework in your early childhood program. These questions encourage you to step back and reflect on your current perspectives surrounding play and learning. What image do you have of young children? How could you rethink the way those perspectives guide your practices?

Imagine the possibilities the revisiting journey framework has to offer. For instance, it can enhance learning by encouraging children to explore their interests and learn at their own pace. It can help you rediscover your own creativity and innovative capacities as you design play ecosystems to support revisiting journeys. When curated and crafted from children's interests, play ecosystems allow children to test hypotheses, make unexpected discoveries, and understand the basic principles and properties of materials and tools through firsthand experiences. Children think critically, supporting their natural desire to learn and make meaning of the world. This, in turn, leads to deeper connections, underpinning supporting children to use revisiting journeys as a tool for lifelong learning.

Joining children on their journeys does not mean serving as experts with all the answers. Instead, you engage children in asking questions. Part of the joy is discovering alongside children. Throughout this book, we will share parallel journeys educators embarked on when supporting children's revisiting journeys. When children are interested in something, you can research with them to learn about the topic. These parallel journeys are opportunities for growth. They allow you to gain new knowledge and insights. The questions that serve as your driving force come from the children. You research to ensure that you have thoughtful ways to support children's journeys, and building your knowledge base opens up the new pathways and possibilities you can offer to children as they ask new questions during their journeys.

It's time to redefine your understanding of play and learning and discover renewed perspectives. The journey may be challenging or messy, but the outcome will be rewarding. Embrace the adventure!

Miriam and Jessie

CHAPTER 1

Defining a Revisiting Journey

As an adult, you know that learning is an essential part of life. For children, learning always takes place through play. Young children constantly explore the world around them, ask questions, and try new things. Taking revisiting journeys is a powerful method children can use to design and guide their learning.

To *revisit* is to reexamine a thought, concept, emotion, or idea. For example, in the picture book *Roxaboxen* by Alice McLerran, a group of children meet every summer to revisit the make-believe town of Roxaboxen. McLerran describes how the children name a scraggly hill Roxaboxen and adorn it with wooden boxes, recyclable materials, ocotillo plants, and cacti. The hill undergoes a wondrous transformation in their minds each summer, ceasing to be a mere hill and becoming a bustling town with streets lined by white stones, a town hall, and ice cream shops. Brought to life by the children's boundless imaginations, Roxaboxen is not a static hill in the desert. It is a dynamic place that evolves with the children's ideas, and imagination—and fierce discussions. It is a place where they learn to adapt, to revisit and revise their projects, and to rebuild the town as their imaginations shift. In this revisiting journey, the children develop their learning dispositions, emotions, and creativity. They explore their capacity for negotiation and become skilled collaborators.

Every child is on their own journey to play and learn. The journey they take is not linear or circular. They may take many turns, go in circles, spiral, or wander on winding roads. Like a captivating story, this journey may have a beginning, multiple middles, and an end. Or it may continue indefinitely, a testament to the endless possibilities of learning. A child may explore an object or use a tool to figure something out. They may get distracted and leave the space, then return later to explore the object and tool again. They may explore it differently, discover new things, and generate new ideas each time. Children's complex journeys tell the story of their individual approaches to learning. The best way to understand children's revisiting journeys is to connect the process to the educator's and children's personal experiences, interests, ideas, and memories.

Can you remember a time when you had to step back from a challenge to reflect, rethink, and rediscover new approaches to find solutions? Stepping back enabled you to come back refreshed, with new ideas and perspectives on how to solve the problem. It allowed you multiple opportunities to prototype and revisit your ideas. Your mistakes in the process guided you to make different decisions until you were satisfied. Children too deserve the opportunity and time to step back and revisit their ideas and work.

A revisiting journey begins with a child's natural curiosity. It's an adventure brimming with questions, explorations, and reflections. In the classic Lewis Carroll book *Alice's Adventures in Wonderland*, Alice, the protagonist, embarks on a truly transformative journey that requires her to reimagine and revisit various situations from a unique perspective. She must trust the characters she encounters and have the courage to test what they offer her, including everything from new foods to extraordinary situations. Alice's curiosity guides her through unexpected discoveries. She comes in and out of adventures, collecting knowledge and applying new information to solve the mysteries she encounters. You have the unique opportunity to foster similar adventures by inviting children to follow their curiosity and revisit, reflect on, and deepen their understanding of the world around them.

As a child engages in inquiry, they create a plan and stay focused on achieving their self-created outcomes. A revisiting journey emerges from a child's self-initiated play and grows as the child's interests evolve and change. As an educator, you play a crucial role in creating curiosity and complexity. A revisiting journey requires you to observe, reflect, map, and respond without providing answers to questions.

When children enter revisiting journeys, they acquire the knowledge they will need as they grow and move through the levels of schooling. They are motivated to speak meaningful sentences to explain their thinking, coming to truly understand new vocabulary and concepts rather than merely repeating a word of the week they have memorized. One of the biggest mistakes the many educational systems have made is breaking tasks down into components; children practice the elements isolated from the whole and focus on memorizing and repeating content that's meaningless without context. For instance, adults may ask children to follow directions to complete an adult-designed craft instead of allowing them to explore an artistic process that interests them. In doing so, adults may turn what would be meaningful and exciting into something pointless and boring—and in the process, prevent children from engaging further out of fear of making mistakes. Imagine what would happen if adults and children alike could view each mistake as an opportunity to start a new revisiting journey.

Long before they begin kindergarten, children's love for learning drives them to generate ideas based on their experiences and understandings about how things work. These early theories (all round objects sink, balls can roll by themselves, my hands make the water cold) are often scientifically inaccurate, but they represent a rudimentary understanding of science concepts across content areas, including physics, chemistry, mathematics, and engineering. Children's curiosity, fueled by their love for learning, leads them to revisit their ideas, exploring and testing their hypotheses with passion and deep interest in discovering new outcomes. As they seek to make sense of their world, young children also reason in ways that are foundational to later scientific thinking.

Understanding children's thinking and their inquiry paths is the key to guiding them toward deeper understanding. Within every revisiting journey are pivoting points at which children's interests shift or their discoveries lead to a new idea, proposal, or question. As an educator, you can use these pivoting points to plan next steps to support the revisiting journey. You can also help children develop a love for learning by questioning and challenging their theories and ideas. A love for learning propels them into an inquiry process. This dynamic cycle of inquiry fostered by adults becomes an integral part of their learning journey, empowering you in your role as guide and facilitator.

Redefining a Learning Moment

The term *teachable moment* is a common one in education. Often, a teachable moment occurs by accident. It can be an unexpected event in day-to-day interactions and activities that engage children's curiosity. An educator uses the event to teach something new to children. Perhaps the educator creates a lesson plan incorporating specific academic expectations. Throughout the interactions, the educator is in control of the learning. The adult sets the tone, and the children follow.

This book proposes a different approach—one in which children are invited to intensely experience objects, materials, and relationships with intentionality and freedom. The revisiting journey framework is grounded in the concept of heutagogy, the art of guiding and supporting interdependent, self-determined learners who thrive from investigating novel experiences. The term *heutagogy* derives from the Greek word *heuriskein*, which means "to discover." As children embark on revisiting journeys, they embrace the freedom to explore and express their thoughts and ideas, they assume responsibility for their learning, and they open themselves to new possibilities and a deeper understanding of who they are and of the world around them.

Shifting from a pedagogical (teacher-led) approach to a heutagogical (learner-led) approach requires patience and commitment. Educators must undertake the work of changing the way they view young children. During this transformational process, remember that it will take time to alter your thinking. Educators are too often pressured to use an educator-directed focus in their programs, requiring children to sit at tables, trace letters, and complete worksheets to prepare for kindergarten. We must transition into an approach that celebrates children's innate abilities and supports their journeys to discovery. It is essential to know yourself before you begin this evolution. You must reflect on your teaching practices and your vision of children to prepare yourself for this reformation.

To fully engage in a revisiting journey, children need to feel free to ask questions, engage in dialogue, and have diverse perspectives. Educators need to integrate democratic ecosystems that encourage dialogue and promote listening and respect. Focusing on democracy versus setting classroom rules supports children's interest in connecting with others and being part of the community. We recognize that to promote equity is to believe that all children come into the world ready to learn, and they do not need to be "readied" for kindergarten.

We want to offer a new way of thinking as we invite you to revisit the idea of learning. We see learning as transformational—a process that is much more profound than memorizing and recalling information taught by adults. At the same time, we want to engage your curiosity and invite you to become a lifelong learner as you engage your curiosity by joining the children in a revisiting journey. Long-lasting learning involves understanding and relating ideas, making connections between prior and new knowledge, thinking independently and critically, and transferring knowledge to new and different contexts. Learning requires you to follow children's revisiting journeys and respond to their wonderment and curiosity.

You shape your understanding of a child by identifying their strengths, learning capacities, and dispositions and by viewing each child as a proficient and imaginative learner. Children learn through their distinct identities. When you accompany children on revisiting journeys, the children serve as your guides, empowering you to respond to their interests and play. You can listen to the children and encourage them to ponder how their ideas enrich the community's learning. You can craft each step of the revisiting journey by incorporating the children's contributions into the design process. In doing so, you nurture identities that evolve, bolster, and cultivate children's agency, paving the way for promising futures.

Learning is not linear or circular. Learning is messy, just as creativity is messy. It builds and compounds on itself. Designing ecosystems where children engage in essential pivoting points (revisiting, rethinking, reflecting, reimagining, rediscovering, redesigning, and redefining) to pursue their theories enables them to gain more profound knowledge and understanding of who they are and of their learning process.

- **Revisiting** allows children to see their ideas, explore them, and gain new understanding and perspective.
- **Rethinking** invites children to generate innovative solutions to old problems with flexibility and agency.
- **Reflecting** moves children from one idea to the next with intention and consideration for different variables. Reflection is the thread that connects ideas into learning.
- **Reimagining** helps children become confident, build critical awareness, and gain the ability to transform and generate change.
- **Rediscovering** brings wonder into children's curiosity. As they discover new approaches or new ways of finding information, they continue to wonder and yearn for more.
- **Redesigning** finds new pathways that lead to more questions and more discoveries. Children take the time to test their prototypes and redesign them, perhaps incorporating new materials to spark new ideas.
- **Redefining** happens when children share and reiterate either verbally or representationally how they figured things out and what they learned.

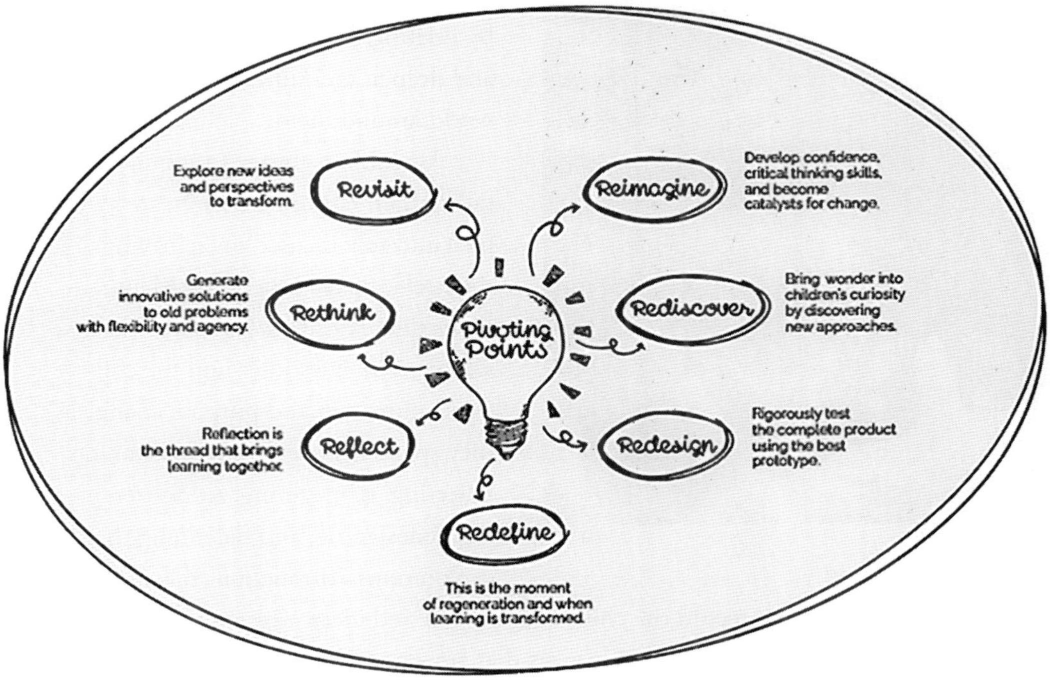

The Revisiting Journeys Framework

A revisiting journey is complex yet rewarding. It takes time and flexibility and requires educators to observe, reflect, map, and respond without providing answers to questions. Instead, educators recognize that in a revisiting journey, children ask questions because they want to know everything and not just the small parts of their investigation. It is supported with a revisiting journeys framework that guides educators' actions and responses. The framework encompasses the following elements:

- identifying how children enter revisiting journeys
- designing responsive play ecosystems
- creating chronicles of revisiting journeys
- developing educators' parallel journeys

Identifying How Children Enter Revisiting Journeys

Children's natural curiosity is the spark that ignites their thrilling journey of discovery and learning. This journey is an adventure brimming with questions, explorations, and reflections. Educators have the unique opportunity to foster and guide children's curiosity by inviting them to revisit, reflect on, and deepen their understanding of the world around them.

As children engage in inquiry to satisfy their curiosity, they create a plan and stay focused on achieving their self-created outcomes. Many times their revisiting journeys lead to asking more questions, and the children's outcomes and purpose change as they spend time revisiting, rethinking, reflecting, reimagining, rediscovering, redesigning, and redefining their explorations. Throughout this process, educators observe and record the children's interests and ideas. They analyze this data to identify specific revisiting journeys that are emerging. For instance, educators notice that children appear to be interested in mixing paint and realize that when they do, new colors appear. As long as children continue to ask questions and revisit the concept of color mixing, a revisiting journey is emerging. Closely observing play guides educators to make decisions that support the children's revisiting journey.

Our research and observations have identified eighteen categories of revisiting journeys. Chapter 2 covers these categories in detail.

Designing Responsive Play Ecosystems

We refer to the classroom as a responsive play ecosystem where relationships are built and maintained. A play ecosystem is more than just a playground or a classroom—it is a complex and dynamic system that mimics the interactions of a natural ecosystem. The children, adults, materials, and physical environment all shape how each child learns and grows in a play ecosystem. A well-designed play ecosystem is a fertile space where the magic of revisiting journeys begins, offering endless opportunities for learning, growth, and imagination. The play ecosystem empowers children, telling them, "You belong here and have the freedom to explore and learn at your own pace and follow your own interests."

The play ecosystem supports children to test hypotheses, make unexpected discoveries, and understand the basic principles and properties of materials and tools through interactive and responsive experiences. This joyful learning process encourages children to think critically, supporting their natural desire to learn and make meaning of the world. This, in turn, leads to deeper connections, underpinning children's ability to use revisiting journeys as a tool for lifelong learning. This process of active participation and reflection paves the way for innovative concepts to emerge, thereby reconstructing a world of possibilities and underscoring the vast potential of our young learners.

The educator, as the architect of play ecosystems, has a crucial role in creating curiosity and complexity. The journeys children undertake inform your teaching practices. As you identify the journeys children enter into, you can create new and different affordances opportunities for children to experiment with during their meaning-making process (the process children use to evaluate and interpret actions, objects, and events based on their previous experience and knowledge). For instance, when you take note of children's continued quest to play "big sibling and baby," you might add more soft materials (blankets, scarves, pieces of fabric) for them to use as props, books to inspire their stories, and unscripted (open-ended) materials for them to incorporate into their narratives.

The early childhood ecosystem can be a place for dialogical interaction, a type of conversation in which participants explore and construct knowledge together. When children engage in this type of dialogue closely linked to their interests, it can positively influence their personal and social identities. In other words, constant respectful and intentional theorizing with young children helps them develop their identities based on their perceptions and understanding of who they are as learners.

Creating Chronicles of Revisiting Journeys

Every revisiting journey is a story that must be told. In this book, we use the term *chronicle* instead of *documentation*. A chronicle implies a detailed approach to capturing the history of a revisiting journey. Since revisiting journeys are constantly in flow, a chronicle helps establish a continuous account of events in the order in which they occur.

Chronicling allows you to bring children's explorations and learning to life, inspiring a sense of purpose and dedication. It tells the story of each child's discoveries, connections, and experiences, showcasing the impact of your work together. It makes their growth and thinking process visible, affirming the importance of your role. Chronicles validate your work as an early childhood educator by showing the relationships between the intentionality of the revisiting journeys heutagogy and your purposeful classroom design, which scaffolds and enhances the development of the whole child. Chapter 5 covers the step-by-step process of chronicling.

You can assess your planning by paying close attention to details you have chronicled. You must observe the relationship between the children and the space to understand and support their journeys. You can act as researchers investigating what is needed in the ecosystem to support children's revisiting journeys and to be flexible in responding to their pivoting points that lead to multiple learning paths.

Developing Educators' Parallel Journeys

Joining children on their journeys does not mean serving as the experts with all the answers. Instead, educators engage children in asking questions. Part of the joy of revisiting journeys is discovering alongside the children. When the children are interested in something, you can research with them to learn about the topic and ensure that you have thoughtful ways to support their journeys. A parallel journey leads you to engage your curiosity as you review the data you collect, research new information, and seek new knowledge and understanding. Building your knowledge base helps open pathways and possibilities you can offer the children as they ask new questions during their journeys.

Discerning whether you see a child entering a revisiting journey takes resolve and a critical eye. You must push aside self-doubt in your ability to recognize these journeys, as well as your preconceived notions about what the children are doing, and instead embrace the unknown and unpredictable. You may believe the children are embarking on a technological exploration of baby carriers only to find that the children have changed directions and created a journey into evaluating their roles as older siblings. These shifts in play may cause you to question your own skills as an educator and researcher. However, you are not just an observer; you are also a collaborator with the children. Realizing this can help you find comfort as you recognize your misperceptions and continue your journey of learning and growth.

The Benefits of Revisiting Journeys

Through play, children develop their identities and build relationships with others, allowing them to see different perspectives and learn valuable social and emotional skills. The benefits of supporting children's revisiting journeys are many and far-reaching. Following are just some of the benefits of revisiting journeys that we have identified. We invite you to explore other benefits as you apply the framework into your programs.

Increasing Children's Learning

When children enter a revisiting journey, they learn because of the pure enjoyment of learning and discovering something new. For instance, when infants acquire language, they babble and curiously wait for a response. They test a new sound, and they delight with each discovery. They are interested in the reactions of the adults in their lives and are motivated to engage their language abilities further. They are learning for the pleasure of learning. Children are motivated to learn when something interests them. Often they do not expect specific answers to their questions; instead, they embrace the unexpected discoveries they encounter as they ask more questions.

The inherent messiness of learning is a powerful catalyst for creativity. By embracing the chaotic and unpredictable nature of the learning process, you open yourself to new possibilities and innovative solutions. It is time to reexamine what it means to learn effectively. Educators must recognize that the path to true understanding and creative brilliance is paved not with order and precision but with the beautiful, messy complexity of exploration and discovery.

In a revisiting journey, learning increases for both children and educators because both review and reconfigure their theories until they have a clearer idea of what they were investigating. As they revisit, they develop a vision of who they are as learners. They explore new dispositions and emotions and they grow as scientists and investigators.

Creating Cultures of Inquiry

You begin to create a culture of inquiry when you are open to exploring and integrating new processes and being guided by children's curiosity. Engaging in a new process requires change, commitment, and patience. It requires you to manage expectations and the disequilibrium that comes from incorrect answers. You are

learning a new language and understanding how children follow their curiosities. You are challenging your thinking and exploring opportunities to integrate new knowledge. As the culture of your classroom changes, you create spaces that embrace the inquiry of revisiting journeys.

Embracing inquiry is about nurturing children's curiosity, a process that goes beyond posing open-ended questions and delivering information. As an educator, you play a crucial role in guiding children on their revisiting journeys. You observe and listen, and most importantly, you foster individual expression, group collaboration, and problem exploration. Questions emerge as children engage in play. You recognize which questions to ask to promote deeper thinking and when to ask them. You intentionally acknowledge that everyone involved in the revisiting journey has an individual and concrete point of view that highlights different ideas.

Learning to Listen

The revisiting journeys framework requires you as an educator to listen and observe deeply to identify children's inquiry. Every step of the revisiting journey is an invitation to listen to children and to understand the multiple ways in which they express their ideas (through art, dramatic play, and verbal and physical communication). As you listen closely, you can better support children in their search for understanding of what they experience.

Since the revisiting journeys framework requires you to become a skilled observer and to notice the different ways in which children express themselves, you also listen to children's theories to discover how they think and question and make connections within their world. The act of listening becomes a dynamic, interactive process that enables meaning making. Your teaching becomes rooted in the belief that listening is less about hearing words and more about fostering genuine understanding and connection. In the article "The Pedagogy of Listening: The Listening Perspective from Reggio Emilia," Carlina Rinaldi emphasizes, "The capacity for listening and reciprocal expectation is an important quality, enabling communication and dialogue, and demands to be understood and supported" (2011, 3). This philosophy underscores the importance of listening as a fundamental human interaction that extends beyond the classroom.

Searching for Meaning

The essence of a child's revisiting journey lies in their personal quest for meaning. From a child's perspective, a revisiting journey is a focused exploration of a question, theory, or problem that stems from their unique interests and ideas. They embark on this journey armed with evidence-based reasoning and creative problem solving, leading them to a conclusion. This captivating process unfolds in their play, art, and authentic conversations with adults and peers, reflecting the profound influence of their personal motivations. For you as an educator, a revisiting journey is born of a deep interest in learning more about the children you care for and educate. Your curiosity is piqued as you observe, listen, and cochronicle the stories of learning.

Enhancing Critical Thinking

A revisiting journey propels children and educators beyond mere curiosity and into critical thinking and understanding. Educators, as the guiding lights, play a pivotal role in this process. You not only encourage children to ask questions but also provide unwavering support, instilling confidence and reassurance throughout the investigation process. Your understanding of when to initiate, when to change direction, and how to create a flexible structure for a revisiting journey is what makes this journey possible. Children need time to build on their curiosity and develop critical thinking. They must be challenged and encouraged to ask questions to expand their knowledge. A revisiting journey promotes the conditions for children to ask questions, listen with intent, and pursue their curiosity as they increase critical-thinking capacities.

Developing a Sense of Self

Revisiting is a powerful tool that helps children gain confidence as they become more aware of their knowledge, skills, and dispositions. As children revisit, they develop a sense of self and reflect on their identity.

Revisiting requires both children and educators to be courageous as they reconceptualize a specific problem or situation. In revisiting journeys, children and educators learn to accept mistakes as opportunities to make meaningful changes.

As you support children's revisiting journeys, you also embark on your own revisiting journey, constantly challenging and expanding your understanding. You dare to embrace any disequilibrium you feel in learning and researching with children rather than directly instructing them. Like Alice, you and the children follow your curiosity even when it takes you down complex rabbit holes. Through this transformative process, you acquire new knowledge and become the protagonists of your learning. Your experiences guide you to grow and embrace change.

As an educator engaged in a parallel revisiting journey, you grow in your practice. Your story of discovery comes to life, and new ideas emerge that lead to deeper thinking and reflection. This is how a revisiting journey perpetuates creativity, opportunity, and accomplishment. This parallel learning journey fosters critical reflection and connection with others, as well as a deep connection to your own process of discovery and growth.

Building Community

Play inspires continuous relationship building between children and adults. In the play, children make meaning of the world, acquire new knowledge, and establish shared values as they negotiate rules and discuss their ideas and theories. The role of adults in this process is crucial as they facilitate the play, ensuring that it remains a safe and enriching experience.

One of the benefits of revisiting journeys is that they help individuals apply shared ideals and values within the ecosystems of their communities. Every member of the community's contribution is not just valued but integral to its growth and development. Each has the freedom to express their thoughts and ideas and build connections. A community is built on the premise that people are social beings who thrive in interactions with other people. Humans seek friendships and learn in the context of social interactions. Individuals feel that they belong when they can follow and share their interests, express their ideas, and have a purpose supported by a strong sense of community and connection to the ecosystem. People learn when their contributions are respected. These are just some of the benefits of revisiting journeys that we have identified. We invite you to explore other benefits as you apply the framework into your programs.

CHAPTER 2

Revisiting Play and Learning

"I want to show my leaf," says Rebecca as she picks her special leaf from her basket. Educator Jessie invites Rebecca to share her leaf with the children. "This is Leafy," Rebecca says. "I found him over—" She points toward a group of trees behind the children. "I brought him to circle 'cuz I wanted everyone to see his little lines. He has little lines on him like my hand." She holds up her hand to show her peers. "Do you have a question?" she asks, looking around at her peers.

Diego inquires, "Where was he?"

Rebecca says, "On the ground."

Malacki adds, "Where his mommy?"

Rebecca responds, "On the tree. Next question."

Maya says, "I think you should draw him."

Rebecca, turning toward educator Jessie, says, "I need to draw him."

Jessie responds, "That's a wonderful idea. Would you like to leave him here with me and you can draw him when you come back to school tomorrow?"

Rebecca nods. Maya then exclaims, "We can all draw him! Jessie, we will need paper and pencils. Oh, and the black thing."

Santiago clarifies, "Magnifying glasses."

This joyous conversation is filled with learning that naturally evolves as children play at leaf collecting. Rebecca is learning that she is a leader and a scientist as she responds to the other children's questions and ideas. Rebecca loves to care for gardens. She is the first to notice the tree is losing leaves, the first to notice the colors of the leaves have changed, and the first to want to explore what hail feels like. She shares theories about why these changes may be happening and enjoys bringing nature items to meeting time. Rebecca is learning that play is learning, and she has many dispositions that help her learn. Play continues to inspire learning in the various revisiting journeys the children engage in throughout the year as they explore who they are, how they learn, and what they can do.

Valuing Play as Learning

The revisiting process is based on the philosophical foundation that play and learning are inseparable and centered on a heutagogy that is deeply attuned to children's ideas and interests. This type of learning not only nurtures children's identities but also sparks their creativity and inspiration, helping them cultivate their understanding of themselves as capable and imaginative learners. It is adults' collective responsibility to create an educational environment that supports and encourages a vision of children as capable constructors of knowledge.

Children who play and explore in an intentionally designed ecosystem focused on inquiry and innovation thrive and develop a love for learning. The research on play as a vehicle for learning is robust. In the book *Play: How It Shapes the Brain, Opens the Imagination, and Invigorates the Soul*, Stuart Brown and Christopher Vaughan (2009) argue that beyond play's role in our fulfillment, its benefits have profound implications for child development, parenting, education, social policy, business innovation, productivity, and even the future of society. Play energizes, eases burdens, and restores humanity and optimism.

Educator and author John Holt (2017) offers an essential perspective on how children learn and perceive the world. In his book *How Children Learn*, he closely examines how children learn, process information, and understand how things function. More importantly, he offers a clear perspective of the brilliance of children. He reiterates that children do not choose to learn just to perform in the future. They decide to do things in the moment and learn through doing. They engage in meaningful ideas and are interested in the pure joy of doing. When their efforts fail, they regroup and continue until they achieve their goal. For example, when infants talk, they want to communicate with other people. Infants babble even though adults do not understand what they are saying; their babbling continues because they think they are communicating. As infants listen and observe other people talking, they communicate better.

A wealth of research on the benefits of play and the profound impact of unscripted materials (often called Loose Parts) on children's development shows a compelling link between play and children's revisiting journeys. The more opportunities children have to fully engage their curiosity and inquiry, the more these trigger the learning process. For children, inquiry means asking questions, exploring possibilities, and asking more questions. There are times when they have a specific outcome in mind, and other times when they don't have a specific goal or seek concrete answers, rather engaging in the process for the pure pleasure of finding unexpected discoveries. Learning flourishes when children create a theory detached from a performance or demonstration for adults. For example, as children play with materials such as Loose Parts, they use them uniquely to represent their ideas. In the process, they learn about themselves and their dispositions for learning. The freedom to play and the unscripted materials help them see themselves as powerful learners.

The Four Tenets of Play-Inspired Learning

To deepen our understanding of the influence of play in all aspects of learning, we have separated learning inspired by play into four equally essential tenets. The tenets are interconnected and operate in unison to create a dynamic and robust educational process that is integrated into the revisiting journeys children take. Together these tenets served as the lens through which we researched and identified the various revisiting journeys covered in this book.

- identity
- praxis
- meaning making
- community

PLAY INSPIRES LEARNING

IDENTITY

- Learning as Being
- Learning as Transformation
- Learning as Becoming

PRAXIS

- Learning as Doing
- Learning as Process
- Learning as Practice

MEANING

- Learn as Experience
- Learning as Freedom
- Learning as Exploration

COMMUNITY

- Learn as Contribution
- Learning as Co-Creators
- Learning as Belonging

Identity

It is crucial for children to recognize and embrace their diverse identities and to feel esteemed for who they are so they see their full potential as learners and human beings. Individual identity (I am capable and have many ideas I can share) and collective identity (I can actively contribute to the community, and my contributions are valued) coexist and influence each other, underscoring the urgency and significance of creating learning communities where children and adults learn from one another and explore similarities and differences. Educators must create spaces that allow children to develop their identities rather than imposing assumptions on them. Educators must be fully present and listen to how children express and represent who they are and how they perceive themselves as individuals and community members.

Educational systems must design opportunities for children to explore their identities based on the following principles:

- Learning as being: Children are unique and have strengths that they use daily. Their experiences and culture guide who they are today.
- Learning as transformation: As children explore their cultural values, capacities, and abilities in a safe ecosystem, they transform and grow.
- Learning as becoming: As children play and learn about their identities, they create a hopeful future for themselves and others.

Reflective Questions

- **What are some of the strengths of the children in your ecosystem?**
- **How do these strengths transform how they learn?**
- **In what ways do children's identities guide them in creating hopeful futures?**

Exploring Identity in Action

Making representations is one way children explore their identities. Mirrors around the room allow children to study themselves and observe their unique characteristics. Educators encourage the children to create representations of themselves using unscripted materials that reflect their features. As the children investigate their individual characteristics, they begin to compare and contrast their features with those of their peers. This ongoing journey emphasizes that children express their identities using different tools and materials. (You can read more about this revisiting journey into representation in chapter 10.)

Praxis

Praxis is the ongoing application of theories to everyday experiences. Praxis is a crucial aspect of learning because it gives children ownership and agency over their decisions and the process of understanding and gaining knowledge. It requires the active participation of both educators and children in making decisions and pursuing interests. Educators play a pivotal role by creating opportunities for children to research, prototype, test, and apply their theories.

Using a revisiting journey approach encourages commitment to the learning process and promotes children's physical movement, communication, exploration, meaning construction, and artistic expression and reflects the following principles:

- Learning by doing: In an ever-changing world, action best achieves understanding. This practical world can only be known when we engage in it.
- Learning as process: The more children test a theory and follow its process, the more they enter into inquiry and learn.
- Learning as practice: To solidify learning, children need ample opportunities to revisit, reflect, redesign, reimagine, and reconstruct.

Reflective Questions

- **In your daily interactions with children, what processes have allowed them to generate, test, and revisit theories?**
- **What opportunities to revisit, reflect, reimagine, and reconstruct could you design into the play ecosystem?**
- **How do children's theories exist in the ecosystem?**

Exploring Praxis in Action

As children go about their day and explore the natural surroundings in the program, they consistently put their theories into practice (praxis). The educators notice that the children are creating circular images and spirals using various materials from nature. They generate different theories about their work and test the theories using a variety of media. They begin with a theory about circles that evolves to include spirals and mandalas. In the process, the children replicate their ideas both outdoors and indoors. They demonstrate thoughtful commitment and interaction as they work together. A sense of altruism and interpersonal relationship develops in the process. The children become in tune with one another's movements and listen thoughtfully to one another's theories and propositions. They give one another permission to trust the creative process. At first the designs are simple. Eventually the children add, change, and modify their designs to make them more complex. The complexity grows as children revisit their theories and explore them from different perspectives, such as drawing, painting, wire sculptures, and natural ephemeral art. (You can read more on the children's praxis through replication in chapter 8.)

Meaning Making

Meaning making is the process by which children interpret situations, events, objects, or conversations in light of their previous knowledge and experience. The ability to make meaning develops over time and through experience. It is a process that continues throughout one's life. Each person enters meaning making from their own perspective and unique point in their meaning-making journey. When children learn through meaning making, they actively engage in problem solving and making sense of a situation. In meaning making, children draw on their history, culture, values, language, and traditions to make meaning of the world. This tenet emphasizes that learning involves identities and emotions, fostering a deeper connection to the learning process.

Since children interpret new experiences and knowledge through their current individual constructions of reality, they may discount or ignore information that doesn't fit their meaning making. Hence, revisiting journeys are essential to continue to make meaning of experiences that did not correlate to earlier understanding.

Meaning making encompasses the following:

- Learning as experience: Children need to engage in multiple experiences to make meaning of their learning.
- Learning as exploration: Children need to explore their thinking, their feelings, and what is happening around them from multiple perspectives before giving meaning to these perceptions.
- Learning as freedom: As children make meaning of their experiences, they learn that they can play and make decisions freely. This process empowers children, allowing them to build meaningful connections with adults and peers.

Reflective Questions

- **How might you design an early childhood play ecosystem that offers multiple opportunities to engage in a variety of experiences that connect to children's realities?**
- **What does learning as freedom mean to you?**
- **How will you support children's freedom to learn and explore in meaningful ways?**

Exploring Meaning Making in Action

While on a class walk, children in the program notice that fallen jacaranda flowers leave color marks on the sidewalk. They become curious and pick up the fallen flowers, rubbing them between their hands to see the stains the flowers leave. The children then step on the flowers on the sidewalk, pounding them into the cement to see if the color will transfer. Noah exclaims, "Look, I am painting!" The children have many questions and hypotheses about how the flowers leave colorful marks on the cement. Rebecca, who loves to garden and likes to document changes in the environment, shares theories about why the flowers are leaving stains on the sidewalk. She says, "The flowers are blue because the rain makes them blue." Kia softly asks, "We don't have a lot of rain, so how can the flowers still be blue?" Always curious, Harper shares her hypothesis: "It kinda has a little paint when you walk on it." The children have a theory, and the educators provide tools and materials to test their hypotheses. They also give children the freedom of time and guidance, based on trust in their abilities and capacities. In this interactive and supportive process, children learn to think beyond the limits of academic learning and are free to become the learners they believe they are. (You can read more about how children make meaning of their surroundings in chapter 7.)

Community

Learning is a reciprocal process that unfolds within the community. As active participants, children not only benefit from their interactions with peers and adults but also contribute significantly to the community. They engage in community-service projects, share their unique perspectives in group discussions, and enrich the community's cultural events. Their strengths, ideas, and interests are valued and recognized. Through these experiences, children gain a deeper understanding of themselves, their environment, and the art of building positive, constructive relationships with others. Learning in community incorporates the following principles:

- Learning as contribution: When children are truly recognized and valued as community members and their contributions are not just honored but also respected, children are empowered to take ownership of their learning journey.
- Learning as cocreating: Children cocreate their learning experiences in relationships with peers and adults. This collaborative approach enhances their learning and fosters a sense of belonging and community.
- Learning as belonging: When children feel they belong, they can learn and support the learning of others.

Reflective Questions

- How do you define *community*?
- What strategies could you use to create a stronger sense of community?
- Why is respecting children's contribution to the community important to create a sense of belonging?

Exploring Community in Action

Children understand that community is part of their identity. When their contributions are valued and respected, children learn—and they begin to see themselves as valuable members of their community.

Threads of fire and firefighters arose in play. The children turned buckets into helmets and ramps (typically used to explore rolling) into hoses. Inspired by these repurposed interpretations, the teachers shone a digital projection of a fire onto a blank space in the classroom. Dillon cried out, "There's a fire in the cube! It's not working, we have to spray faster!" Broc responded, "We have to spray it out!"

To extend the exploration of fire, we offered images of fires and videos of the children's dramatic play alongside red, orange, yellow, and brown colored pencils. Dillon and Nico recalled the vivid colors of fire:

> **Dillon: "When the wildfires were in the air, there was smoke. I'm trying to remember what it looked like. The fire burned, and then there was smoke."**
>
> **Nico: "This is what yellow fire looks like."**
>
> **Dillon: "Orange is the wildfire color."**

This story about community continues in chapter 11.

A Robust Research Behind Revisiting Journeys

After years of observing how children follow their curiosity to explore and make meaning of their thinking, Miriam was eager to understand what motivates children's inquiry and how their inquiry promotes learning. In 2020 she spent a sabbatical year studying how children enter into inquiry. She began conducting academic research to answer the following questions:

- How do children enter into inquiry?
- What support do children need to enter the inquiry process?
- How may educators facilitate or hinder the inquiry process?
- What is the role of the environment in supporting the inquiry process?
- What is the role of the materials in supporting the inquiry process?

As part of the sabbatical, Miriam conducted a comprehensive and meticulous literature review—analyzing over one hundred books and academic journal articles on play, learning, and inquiry—to gain a more in-depth understanding. She watched one hundred videos of children playing in early childhood programs throughout the country and examined 514 pieces of documentation from three preschool classrooms at the Center of Gravity preschool in Pleasant Hill, California, highlighting children's interests and adult-child interactions. Miriam meticulously tabulated, recorded, and analyzed the data with a focus on the conditions that support children to initiate the inquiry process. This thorough data collection process ensures the credibility and reliability of the findings.

Miriam identified eighteen categories of revisiting journeys that engage children's inquiry and can serve as a lens to determine children's curiosities, dispositions, and learning strategies. The research findings guided Miriam and Jessie's development of the revisiting journey framework. By identifying the various revisiting journeys in children's play, we empower educators and curriculum developers to better support children's learning by designing ecosystems, curriculum, and interactions around these observations. The concept of revisiting journeys also guides how we assess and reflect on our practices. We recognize that as educators, we have a moral imperative to provoke and design opportunities for children to revisit and reflect on their play. We have learned that revisiting journeys create a collective momentum for reclaiming joy and protecting children's right to be inquisitive.

It is time to document how society has created a disastrous gap in thinking about play, inquiry, innovation, equity, and social justice that directly impacts opportunities for children and their future. Currently, many educational systems focus on *what* children need to learn and not on *how* they learn. Our view is that by switching the paradigm from the *what* to the *how*, education can better support children's growth and development.

The revisiting journeys framework provides a practical lens to observe how children learn through play and what strategies educators can use to support how children learn. In part 2 of this book, we present how educators in various early childhood programs have used the revisiting journeys framework to identify and guide children's interests and inquiry.

Types of Revisiting Journeys

During our research we identified the following revisiting journeys:

1. Learning through curiosity: Children explore new materials, create theories, and pursue answers based on their interests and their need to know more deeply.
2. Learning through technological exploration: Children search for new knowledge through constructing, designing, developing prototypes, and testing their hypotheses. They test their ideas through construction in the block space or represent their thinking through an art process.
3. Learning through replication: Children copy other children's work, imitate movements and actions, or replicate things they find in books or in the community. Replication can also be seen in children's need to read the same book repeatedly.
4. Learning through representation: Children search for knowledge by representing their ideas, experiences, thinking, interests, and thoughts with symbolic play and art. This includes using imagination to dream and create hopeful futures.
5. Learning through analysis and evaluation: Children search for knowledge based on how materials function and work together, exploring the affordances the materials offer. Children connect and disconnect objects or use materials in various ways, such as combining them.
6. Learning through history: Children make connections through the knowledge found in artifacts and people. Children are curious about their stories, identities, cultures, and roles in their families and communities.
7. Learning through logico-mathematical and scientific thinking: Children acquire knowledge about quantity, numbers, and spatial relationships as they engage in exploration of unscripted materials and nature, spending time in classification, comparison, and data analysis.
8. Learning through inductive reasoning: Children acquire knowledge by predicting, forecasting, and hypothesizing what will happen next, reaching conclusions by going from the specific to the general. Children sometimes represent inductive reasoning in symbolic play.
9. Learning through metacognition: Children become aware of their thinking process and learn to regulate their thoughts by modifying them, thinking about their thinking. They incorporate their thoughts into their play, art, and behavior.

10. Learning through power: Children explore and act out feelings of dominance and control through play. They use power to understand the limits of their strengths, explore safety, learn about limits, and solve social interaction problems. They thrive by taking risks and challenging limits and rules.
11. Learning through collaboration: Children engage in inquiry through their relationships with other children and adults. They observe and contribute to a community project. Through collaboration, children share their ideas, listen to other people's ideas, and learn who agrees and disagrees with their viewpoints. They enjoy the process with passion and enthusiasm.
12. Learning through democracy: Children hold innate empathy and concern for others and thrive in their ability to help and engage in social justice. Their play often follows a caring or saving theme.
13. Learning through negotiation: Children show the ability to read and understand people's cues and apply this understanding in negotiating to meet their needs, all while recognizing that other people may have different perspectives. Children ask questions to learn more about what they want and need.
14. Learning through physicality: Children move or use their bodies to deepen their knowledge of how things work and how they can control their environment.
15. Learning through interpretation (descriptive and expressive language): Children communicate and defend what they know and think. They make meaning of their thinking and gain understanding of what they do and the processes they engage in to solve a problem by analyzing it as they verbally describe what they do. The Russian psychologist Lev Vygotsky described this self-talk as a guide to cognitive development (1978). Children also use expressive and descriptive language to reflect on their understanding of their thoughts. This interpretation process leads to metacognition (thinking about thinking).
16. Learning through story making: Children are natural storytellers, and they define their personhood and their identities through their stories about their wonderings, playful inquiries, successes, strengths, and capacities. Thoughtfully observing how children discover and make meaning of what they see, notice, and explore can help educators understand children's self-identity creation as a powerful process that propels development.
17. Learning through art: Children use art media to increase knowledge, draw connections between concepts, and create original ideas, representations, and designs utilizing various art media. They prefer to communicate their thoughts by drawing, painting, designing, and sculpting.

18. Learning through nature: Children gain knowledge of science and natural systems and how they influence human interactions. Children must be in direct contact with nature, a concept known as *biophilia*. Biophilia was first introduced as a human personality trait by German psychologist Erich Fromm (1964) and later by American biologist Edward O. Wilson (1984). Fromm and Wilson agree that biophilia has a biological basis and that it is fundamental to develop harmonious relationships between humans and the biosphere. Because nature influences human brain development, it is essential in early childhood ecosystems.

NOTE: These revisiting journey types are not learning styles and should not be used to teach concepts through direct instruction. Instead, they are observations of how children explore and make meaning of their world. The journey types serve as tools to support the design of early childhood play ecosystems that give children opportunities to control their play and learning.

Educators play a crucial role in facilitating revisiting journeys. As children embark on revisiting journeys, they follow their curiosity. When educators systematically observe children and reflect on what they learn from the children's learning, they can foster a collaborative learning environment. This collaboration leads to the creation of new knowledge, which in turn leads to increased knowledge and more engagement that ultimately benefit children, making educators and children feel more connected and building community.

CHAPTER 3

Ecosystems as the Foundations for Children's Revisiting Journeys

An ecosystem is a community of interacting organisms within a shared physical environment. Humans are part of this interconnected system, and they share the space with flora, fauna, inorganic matter (such as rocks and metals), and natural forces (such as the flow of water or fire or the chemistry of photosynthesis). These elements link together and interact as a complex web of life. An early childhood classroom or learning space functions like an ecosystem. In the classroom ecosystem, everything is interconnected, and these connections influence the interactions there.

We refer to the classroom or learning space as a play ecosystem where relationships are built and maintained. It is a complex and dynamic system that mimics the interactions of a natural ecosystem. The children, adults, materials, and physical environment shape how each child learns and grows in a play ecosystem. Through play, children develop their identity and build relationships with others, allowing them to see different perspectives and learn valuable social and emotional skills. A well-designed play ecosystem is a fertile space where revisiting journeys begin and continue, offering endless opportunities for learning, growth, and imagination. This play ecosystem empowers children, telling them, "You belong here. You have the freedom to explore and learn at your own pace and follow your own interests."

The play ecosystems educators curate and design shape children's explorations and thinking, sparking their innate curiosity. When curated and crafted from the children's interests, play ecosystems allow children to test hypotheses, make unexpected discoveries, and understand the basic principles and properties of materials and tools through interactive experiences. This joyful learning process encourages children to think critically, supporting their natural desire to learn and make meaning of the world. This, in turn, leads to deeper connections, underpinning children's ability to use revisiting journeys as a tool for lifelong learning.

Often, educators spend time at the beginning of the school year designing their classroom ecosystems. But instead of designing based on what you think helps children, you could start with a blank canvas, and as you come to know the children you could revisit and redesign the space as relationships build and a new culture of inquiry develops.

A play ecosystem incorporates the following components:

- the physical space
- the socio-emotional space
- the temporal space

The Physical Space

The physical space is a realm for exploration and experimentation, a magical place where creativity and innovation spring from the cultural DNA of its inhabitants. The indoor and outdoor parts of the space are designed for flexibility and responsiveness to emerging revisiting journeys. The elements of the space are interconnected, and they interact to facilitate children and educators living, learning, and researching together. The space fosters harmony and nurtures creative flow through flexible boundaries that allow children to go deeper into their investigations, eliminating time constraints and expanding opportunities to play. Open communication and interdisciplinary collaboration allow creativity to flourish. There is a sense of belonging and the freedom to be authentic. Educators allow children to take calculated risks and test their capacities. The space creates a sense of well-being, cultural representation, and belonging that is essential to revisiting journeys.

The following properties define the physical space:

- sensory: qualities experienced through the senses—shape, line, texture, harmony, color, space, light, sound, and smell
- structural: organization of the space to promote flow, unity, balance, movement, and expression
- natural: access to natural elements, which increases a sense of well-being
- technical: integration of technology to facilitate immersion and support active engagement and chronicling of revisiting journeys

- expressive: use of diverse media (visual arts, performance and dramatic play, music, writing, filmmaking, and so on) to facilitate the exploration, representation, and replication of ideas and interest
- cultural: opportunities to represent and explore individual and group identities

The Socio-Emotional Space

The socio-emotional space is designed to respond to and nurture children's feelings and how children express those feelings. It invites collaboration and peaceful interactions. We propose anchoring the socio-emotional space in empathy, curiosity, and harmony. To amplify these qualities, educators must recognize children's strengths and meet their needs. Respect for the revisiting process reduces competitive, comparative, and commercialized tendencies. Collaboration, permission, and time take precedence instead. Adults' and children's mindsets do not limit exploration. Instead, the ecosystem and people invite change, mystery, and unexpected discoveries. The routines and rituals are meaningful and designed to be responsive to children's unique ways of being. Mistakes are not only embraced but also celebrated, as they provide the necessary conditions to reimagine and discover new possibilities, instilling a sense of confidence in the learning process.

When a play ecosystem is set up with the socio-emotional space in mind, it encourages compassion and respect for individuals and shared tools and materials. There is mutual stewardship of individual and collective processes. Every inhabitant of the play ecosystem can find the balance inside themselves that they need to emerge with energy and commitment to the individual and collective process.

Designing spaces anchored in empathy, ethics, and trust promotes deeper connections and interactions. The revisiting journeys framework gives children and adults permission to be vulnerable, make connections, and release energy in ways that allow them to grow, transform, and create with passion and commitment to themselves and others.

The Temporal Space

The temporal space—which consists of the daily schedule and rhythm of interactions, routines, and rituals—facilitates the revisiting process. Educators notice the pivoting points in children's inquiries and give permission to close a revisiting journey or continue the exploration. The schedule avoids interrupting children's journeys. It is designed around three major anchors: welcoming the day, gathering as a group, and saying goodbye.

Welcoming the children is relaxed and flexible. The day begins with indoor and outdoor play, allowing children and families to arrive without being rushed. There is a designated space for families to gather and meet one another. Families can opt to stay for a while and help transition their children into the flow of the day. A plethora of explorations await, including books, art experiences, and an inviting sand and mud area for messy play. This exciting array of learning opportunities, combined with a flexible arrival schedule, allows educators to connect with the children and their families by being fully present without rushing to start teaching.

The community holds a group gathering to discuss ideas and recent adventures and to address questions and concerns. The conversations may be surprising, and the children participate with excitement and curiosity. Sometimes educators introduce a new idea, tool, or material. Other times the children bring questions and curiosities. We see a group gathering as a learning community collaboratively engaged in a journey. Group gatherings connect individual and collective perspectives, fostering a strong sense of community. Individuals are flexible enough to both learn from and question one another, promoting a sense of shared responsibility. In group gatherings, children and educators share findings and knowledge, fostering a culture of mutual learning. They discuss mistakes and consider alternate solutions, promoting a sense of collective problem solving. The gatherings are grounded in the message "I trust you, I am interested, and I want to know more."

Saying goodbye is not just a formality; it is a crucial part of a child's emotional development. Humans need closure to the time they spend together. Intentional goodbyes, guided by parents and educators, help children build inner comfort. As children wrap up the day, they rely on knowing that a project they started can be completed the next day. They know their friends will gather again to play together. A ritual of saying goodbye creates a transition from the program to home. Educators can invite families to linger as they pick up their children. The children enjoy a few minutes to show their work and share with their family what they did. Goodbyes can be relaxed and enjoyable. Life is filled with goodbye moments. Some goodbyes are temporary, and others are permanent. Saying goodbye helps children appreciate time spent with others and accept their losses. A goodbye helps end one experience while opening space for new ones.

Designing Play Ecosystems

When designing a play ecosystem, one must reflect on the interplay of all of the elements in it: the materials, the tools, the children, the educators, the families, the classroom culture, the daily rhythms and routines, and the community as a whole. High-quality play ecosystems are designed with the children at the center, affording them the opportunity to take charge of their own learning and supporting their interests and developmental needs. Children can discover new possibilities in play ecosystems and make new connections based on their interests and theories.

Observation lies at the heart of design. Thoughtful teachers observe young children throughout the day, taking notes and documenting all the languages children use, both verbal and nonverbal, to communicate their wants and needs. Observation and reflection allow educators to formulate questions about what the children may be trying to discover and form theories about what journeys the children may be entering. Educators use this information to make design decisions, such as reimagining spaces to incite deeper exploration and curating materials and tools to prompt further engagement and new threads of inquiry.

Throughout our time as early childhood educators, we have used many strategies to document our observations of young children. We have found that using a combination of the following forms of documentation is most effective in supporting the design of high-quality play ecosystems. All observation notes must show the date, the precise location indoors or outdoors, and the names of the children involved to best support intentional and purposeful design decisions.

- Handwritten notes: Take notes throughout the day, and then review them when making planning decisions for the next day. It is best to write in a notebook, as notes on loose sheets of paper or sticky notes can get lost. Notes written in a secure, consistent place allow you to build the habit of writing your observations while keeping your thoughts organized. Describe what the children are doing and how they are doing it. Be specific. Write down the conversations you overhear from the children. Write their exact words. Do not attempt to fix the children's grammar in your notes, as their grammatical errors give you insight into their development.
- Photos: While a picture can share a lot of information, it captures only a moment in time. Notes and captions—often simple to add digitally—are essential to round out the story. Children are sharing ideas, engaging in conversations, and playing. Their nonverbal communication cannot be noted through just a picture.
- Videos: Tablets and smartphones make capturing videos easier than ever. Begin recording when you witness an interesting interaction in progress. Another strategy is to place the recording device in a particular space (for example, propped on a shelf) to record whatever happens to occur in front of it. This allows you to capture vital information while remaining available to the group at large.
- Audio recordings: Audio recordings can capture the dialogue during meeting times and small groups. You can place the recording device on a table, a shelf, or next to your own body. With the advancement of artificial intelligence, various tools are available to transcribe recordings.

- Note: Remember to get permission from the families to photograph, film, and collect children's artifacts to use in chronicling the children's journeys.

Jessie shares how her experiences with and connection to the framework of the revisiting journey influence her approach to designing a play ecosystem:

> When I began my work as a director, I had a variety of ideas about the type of program I wanted to create. While children were at the center of my vision, I understood that many other interconnected elements also needed to be addressed to bring the vision to life. I wanted to establish a program where the children could explore and discover the world. I wanted the children to feel secure in testing their ideas and sharing their thoughts. I wanted the children's interests to serve as our curriculum. The play ecosystem had to be formed by creating a collective vision for the program. The space needed to be designed to invite the exchange of ideas, perspectives, and approaches.
>
> I knew that this meant I needed to find early childhood educators who were not afraid to take risks, who would support and celebrate children's inquiries, and who understood the importance of observation and acting as a researcher joining the children in their revisiting journeys. I knew that I needed to work with staff who understood the importance of setting ego aside, who knew the importance of allowing the children to discover, who saw the role of the educator as a researcher as opposed to an all-knowing deity prescribing the children's learning and attempting to control their thinking. This didn't mean allowing the children to do whatever they wanted without consequence, a common misconception that I had observed throughout my career as an early childhood educator. Rather, this meant finding educators who truly understood what it meant to be intentional in their thoughts, actions, and words.
>
> Being intentional would be what defined our program. We would observe children intentionally. We would take the time to notice what the children were doing. What conversations were they having? What words were they uttering? What were they focusing on? How were they using the materials and tools provided? How were they interacting with one another in the spaces? We would ask ourselves these questions to ensure that each space we created had purpose and intention while remaining rooted in the children's interests and messages. In this process, we would generate play ecosystems, spaces with possibilities for the children to enter, revisit, rethink, reflect, reimagine, rediscover, and redefine their ideas and prototypes. These play ecosystems would act as conduits for revisiting journeys that could be built upon, expanded, and revisited in new ways over the years.

We use observation when designing spaces to support children's journeys and play. I pay close attention to what the children are doing in the space. I look at what materials they select and how they use the materials. I also notice what they are not using. I take pictures and videos to help me in my planning. I record their conversations and questions. Sometimes I do this simply by writing notes; other times I use audio recordings that I later transcribe.

Reflective Questions

- What play ecosystems are in your classroom? In your program as a whole?
- How do you use the outdoors and nature in your play ecosystems?
- What systems do you use to create effective play ecosystems?
- What approaches have you used that opened up new possibilities and supported your growth as an educator?
- What strategies have you used that need more attention and focus to be effective?
- How do you evaluate the play ecosystems in your classroom?
- What types of revisiting opportunities do your ecosystems offer?

As an educator, your understanding and planning for children's revisiting journeys are enriched by your personal experiences. Your planning may involve a process of trial and error, and your observations of the children are filtered through your unique lens. This lens can influence how you interpret the meaning behind the children's play scenarios; it means that you might be surprised by the directions children take. We encourage you to embrace the possibility of change, knowing that you may need to adjust unscripted materials and affordances you have provided. This could be because you guessed incorrectly or because the children have found different interests, leading them to new revisiting journeys. Rather than feeling discouraged, you can view such happenings as learning opportunities, taking this new knowledge with you as you return to your planning and determine your next steps.

Educator Tonya shares her story of how she utilizes observation and reflection to guide her decisions in supporting children's revisiting journeys:

My approach to working with young children is, first and foremost, to view them as competent and capable. I see my ethical duty as one in which I support children's innate curiosity and love of learning by providing them with freedom of choice and exploration. I encourage them to test their own theories and make their own discoveries. I do this by stepping back and observing how the children interact with the physical space (the materials and tools I've provided in the indoor and outdoor spaces) and the socio-emotional space (how the children interact with one another and me, their teacher). I provide affordances to the children in the play ecosystem and attempt to capture the manner and means in which the children make use of this time and space. I do this primarily through video and audio recordings. (I am not a fast writer and found that using recordings worked best for me.) In this way, I can relive the experiences I saw the children engage in earlier in the day and use them to guide me in my design decisions.

I try to view the children's engagement and interactions through a lens of curiosity. I ponder what they might be searching for and what unscripted materials I can change to support this journey in our classroom's play ecosystem. In this process, there are still expectations for the children regarding how to safely and respectfully engage with the space, their peers, and the materials. In my experience, children thrive in this style of learning environment, as they have the confidence to explore and an understanding of the boundaries. Due to clear communication with the children, I am able to observe and document their journeys. I can step back and observe the children rather than running around and policing their actions.

With the many competing demands on my time (licensing, funding, and so forth), it can be hard to quiet my mind to truly see and hear the children. One trick I use to do this is taking a deep breath. I imagine in my exhale that I am breathing out all the external pressures and breathing in all the joys that accompany engaging with and observing children. Once centered, I can do the work of observing the children to determine how to redesign the play ecosystem based on what the children's words, actions, and inactions are telling me. By taking the time to be present with the children, we design our play ecosystem with intentionality. The designs are based on the children's own questions and inquiries.

Educators need protected time to gather and reflect together. Reflective time and opportunities to share ideas and play together must be considered as schedules are created. When the program values this time as necessary to promote growth and development, there is a commitment to integrate and protect reflective time in the schedule. This may require shifting other things around. Adults who are flexible and able to go with the flow are more relaxed and attuned to the rhythm of the

interactions and the revisiting journey's process. A temporal schedule that embraces the gift of time helps develop solid attachments and connections.

Jessie reflects on the importance of providing time to educators in early childhood programs:

The Center of Gravity in Pleasant Hill, California.

> Time is always an educator's biggest challenge. With the constant pressures and demands, it can be hard to slow down enough to be truly present with the children. It sounds easy, but it takes a lot of work in practice. Ensuring that educators have the time to do this is crucial.
>
> As an administrator, I recognize the importance of planning time. This allows the educators to brainstorm and collaborate, which are skills we want to encourage for the children in our care. Suppose the educators in our program are afforded this opportunity to commune with colleagues and think critically. How will they then foster these abilities in young children? Through practicing these skills firsthand, educators become versed in their understanding of how to scaffold this crucial learning in their play ecosystem.
>
> Creating opportunities for planning on a tight operating budget takes work. However, recognizing its importance, I have reimagined our program and prioritized planning time. Teaching dyads meet weekly to share their insights, analyze the data with one another, and plan for the upcoming week.
>
> I meet with the leads once a week to collaborate and determine ways to support one another. We look at the

interests and actions seen in the children's play and discuss how to support them. What unscripted materials could we add, change, or remove to foster the children's curiosities and extend their engagement and learning? We note which spaces the children visited frequently and which spaces the children seemed to ignore. We make alterations around these observations. A continuous cycle of observation and reflection informs our planning process.

In Jessie's program, the educators plan the curriculum and environment together. They fine-tune the play ecosystem by homing in on the interests of the children. They think critically about the children's communication through their behavior, actions, and inactions.

The play ecosystem permits children and adults to freely explore ideas, relationships, and theories. It provides a sense of belonging and the freedom to be authentic. The space invites the exchange of ideas, perspectives, and approaches. There children can wonder, play, and find joy. Choices and conditions are not arbitrary or performative. Instead, they are planned to be playful and flexible without expectations for specific deliverables.

Reflective Questions

- **What are the unique challenges your program poses to designing a play ecosystem?**
- **How do you approach these unique challenges of your program structure?**
- **Who could support you in discovering the meaning behind children's behavior? How would you use this information to support children in their revisiting journeys?**
- **What are you noticing the children doing in the play ecosystem? What are the children saying while on this journey?**
- **Are there other unscripted materials and tools you could offer to deepen the children's journeys and encourage their revisiting process?**

Parallel Journey

CHAPTER 4

Embarking on Educator Parallel Journeys

As an educator, you are tasked with creating a love of learning in young children that puts them on a lifelong path of continued growth. Guiding the revisiting process requires thoughtful actions and reflective decisions from you. Your understanding and planning for children's revisiting journeys are enriched by your personal experiences. Embarking on parallel journeys that allow you to hypothesize and develop educated guesses about young children's own revisiting journeys supports your planning. Parallel journeys create opportunities for you to constantly reflect and change your practices, thus creating a culture of inquiry where you and children partner to create a robust play and learning ecosystem. A parallel journey is not a solitary path, but one that encourages you to focus on children's curiosity and inquire about children's interests. It's a journey that thrives on questioning, reflection, and reimagining learning.

Be careful not to use stereotypical learning tropes to define the children's journeys. This means that you must be attentive to the many ways children communicate with you, such as direct verbal communication, conversations with their peers that you overhear, art representations, and behaviors and actions you see. In this communication, you learn the children's interests and needs. You can then determine how best to serve as a coresearcher and collaborator to guide the children on their journeys and ensure you meet these communicated objectives and desires.

The Actions of a Parallel Journey

Your parallel journey as an educator encompasses the actions you take alongside children to deepen your own understanding of the theories and topics the children are exploring. These actions include:

- action research
- adult play
- community partnerships
- chronicling

Action research occurs when you embark on your own research about a topic. To guide children's revisiting journeys, you must research and learn along with them. Research piques your curiosity and lets you grow as an educator and human. Doing research is probably one of the most satisfying parts of a revisiting journey. For example, when children are testing theories about pigmentation, you reflect on their actions and find resources to support their deeper learning and understanding. This is the moment when, as an educator, you must learn as much as you can about color theory. This learning might include finding books that explain color theory and connecting with local artists who experiment with pigmentation and are willing to share their knowledge with you, the children, or both.

American education philosopher John Dewey (1938) stressed the importance of learning by doing. He argued that in an ever-changing practical world, we can only know through action. Applying this concept to your early childhood education program means that the actions you carefully choose and the praxis (putting theory into action) you accomplish will create tangible positive change in children's lives and educational experiences.

You engage in **adult play** when you explore the materials you are planning to offer to children. Often you may think of the play ecosystem as a space for children. While this is true, it is also a space for adults. You as an educator are part of the play ecosystem. Therefore, it is vital for you to feel comfortable in the space. One way to help grow your confidence and build your comfort is to engage with materials, letting go of your preconceived notions about what a material and tool can be used for and instead embracing it as if for the first time.

In play, you as an educator theorize, test, experiment, and investigate new perspectives and methods for interacting with the material and tools. You attempt to discover the different languages the material uses to communicate. You search for the relationships between the material and tools. You welcome the materials and tools into your creative world. You embrace the new and unknown possibilities that arise from your play. You attempt to see the world through the eyes, hearts, and minds of children.

Only when you understand the affordances that materials and tools provide can you offer them to the children. This deep knowing allows you to curate the unscripted materials (Loose Parts) provided in the play ecosystem. By understanding the attributes of materials and experimenting with them yourself, you can unlock new potential and deepen your understanding.

Your **community partnerships** may include finding local individuals and organizations who support the children's lines of inquiry. You can put out an invitation to families for their partnership, participation, and expertise. Additionally, you can seek out local resources that will provide an enriching experience. These resources could include local museums, garden centers, community centers, and more—the possibilities are limited only by the interests of the children.

Chronicles, as visual narratives, play a crucial role in documenting the history of a project or research. They make your thinking, reflections, and research visible, thereby making the learning process tangible. At the start of each parallel journey, it's beneficial to design a wall that will hold the chronicles of your process. There's no limit to your creativity in this. The key is to focus on telling the story of how each step of your process unfolds, as this will significantly benefit your project.

Chronicling makes learning relevant by showing connections between concepts and real-world applications, sparking a sense of discovery and curiosity. It helps you to find the *why* behind the *what*. It helps you answer these questions: What is the children's interest in this project? Why is this interesting? How can we support the process? How much do we know? What do we need to learn? What research do we need to conduct? Are there any gaps that we can fill?

When you engage in action research, adult play, community partnerships, and chronicling, you are embarking on your own journey alongside children. It is important that you recognize that you are not an expert on every topic. You must embrace learning with the children. When you view yourself as a lifelong learner, you are able to set aside ego and instead join the children in pursuit of knowledge. The reflections and actions you take while you attempt to understand children's theories serve as your own parallel journey.

When educators spend time to create the conditions for revisiting, children spend more time replicating and interpreting their own ideas and thinking. Your parallel journeys also help you question when and how much you should intervene in how children learn and how they enter into inquiry. You know that to better support the revisiting journey, you need to collect robust data, ask questions, and closely examine the evidence of your work. Parallel journeys allow you to understand how children learn instead of focusing on what they need to know. Parallel journeys help early childhood educators in the following ways:

1. You recognize what you don't know and what you need to learn.
2. You redefine your role as a learner and not a holder of knowledge.

3. You find the joy of researching and learning.
4. You build efficacy that sparks your curiosity and keeps you questioning and wanting to learn more.
5. You create a culture of inquiry to bridge the opportunity gap for young children and to create play ecosystems that promote equity.

Parallel Journeys in Practice

Jessie shares her experience implementing parallel journeys as a director of an early childhood program:

> Something I noticed when working with my team was that each educator had their own strengths and levels of comfort in play. Some educators loved working with different unscripted materials. Others found them intimidating. They shared that they weren't sure how to use them. They didn't know how to incorporate them into their practice. They questioned how to introduce them to the children.
>
> I wanted all the educators to feel confident and comfortable embracing this work. Rather than having staff/team meetings filled with continuous policy reminders and superfluous information that could be an email, we had reflective meetings. We spent that time collaborating and engaging. I would meet with each teaching dyad ahead of our full team meeting. I would ask them questions about what they had noticed the children saying and doing. I would then curate a plethora of unscripted materials to bring to our full team meeting for adult play. During the meeting, one teaching dyad would share their observations of the children in their classroom. They would provide their theories of what the children were curious about. Their colleagues would also share their own ideas, posing questions to clarify information and provide different thought perspectives. I would then invite the educators to select different materials that they thought would support the children in their journeys. We would spend the time engaging with the materials, writing down the affordances and potential pathways that the unscripted materials could be used in the children's journeys.
>
> At the end, we would reflect together. The educators would share why they selected the materials they did, how they thought these materials would enhance the children's journeys, and what they discovered through their own use of the materials. I found that this style of meeting helped the educators gain confidence in their own planning. They no longer worried about whether their offerings were going to be successful. Instead, they embraced the journey. They began to understand and value the trial and error that goes along with

this work. They stopped viewing their misses as failures. Instead, they saw their misses as opportunities to dive deeper and revisit their own work. They embraced their own parallel journeys!

Parallel Journey

Jessie shares a reflection about parallel journeys:

> When designing spaces, I immerse myself in them. I travel back in time to find my three-year-old self. I invite her to join me. I have her help me curate the design elements and features. I encourage her to engage and play with the materials. I ask her what story she would want to tell. I follow her lead and am transported into a space of curiosity. I research to discover the affordances of the materials. I ask, "What are this material's physical properties? What are its limits and boundaries? What are the possibilities this material might provide?" Understanding the materials is vital to supporting children's journeys. In growing my own knowledge, I am better able to support the children.

Tonya's Parallel Journey

Educator Tonya shares her story of how she engages in parallel journeys and community partnerships:

> I love learning alongside the children. Once I have a theory about their curiosities, I get to work. I brainstorm what I already know about the topic and reflect on whether this aligns with the children's curiosities. I discuss with colleagues and research resources to support the children's line of inquiry. Specifically, I love to look for local partners. I have connected with museums, garden centers, local artists, local grocery stores, and even the local post office. Through these partnerships, I've had guest speakers come in and share their knowledge with the children. We have even had field trips to visit their establishments. Some were within walking distance, making visits easy to do during school hours. For others, we made arrangements with families to meet at the locations outside of school hours.
>
> One of my favorite partnerships is with the Natural History Museum. I reach out and schedule a time to meet with the museum curator. I usually share in my communication what I believe the children are interested in. When I arrive, she has materials ready for me. She walks me through the curation, explaining why and how they are

appropriate for our line of inquiry. She educates me on these materials so that I can then share them with the children.

A parallel journey is not a solitary path, but rather one that encourages educators to focus on their curiosity and inquiry about children's interests. It's a journey that thrives on questioning, reflection, and reimagining learning. It's a journey that necessitates collaboration, research, and shared learning. Collaboration makes visible the intentional planning that guides parallel journeys.

When you are diving into unfamiliar territory, your thinking may feel messy at first. You may be unsure of where to start or how to proceed. This discomfort is a natural part of the learning process. As an educator, you must learn to trust the process of inquiry and be comfortable with the uncertainty it brings. Just like a child, you can expect to take steps forward without knowing where they will lead you. The more you know, the more you gain comfort and confidence in your knowledge.

The parallel journeys you embark on as you guide children in their own revisiting journeys encourage you to think deeply about your values and to give yourself the freedom to grow in your role as an educator. Most importantly, parallel journeys give you the power to question policy and advocate for children's play rights. We invite you to consider your parallel journeys and to embrace a heutagogy that leads to sustainable change.

Reflective Questions

- **How could you incorporate parallel journeys into your heutagogy?**
- **What steps could you take to begin your own parallel journeys alongside children?**
- **What resources do you have that could support you in taking a parallel journey?**
- **Which type of educator parallel journey (action research, adult play, community partnerships, and/or chronicling) are you most comfortable with? Why?**
- **Which type of educator parallel journey do you need to spend more time with? Why?**

"Spinners"

CHAPTER 5

Chronicles as Collaboration

Chronicling the stories of young children's revisiting journeys in your early childhood program is essential. The school year is busy. Growth, development, and change occur quickly. It's easy to overlook where the children began when they first arrived in your care. You may forget the leaps and bounds they have taken in their learning. Starting the year by capturing photos, videos, and dialogue from the children can help you mark and identify the beginning of a revisiting journey. It allows you to see how the journey evolves over time and how the children learn and grow.

We encourage you to reconceptualize your understanding of documentation as a chronicle. A chronicle is a detailed approach to capturing and telling the story of a revisiting journey. Since a revisiting journey is constantly flowing, a chronicle helps establish a history—a continuous, chronological account of events. A chronicle makes these experiences and learning visible and informs planning. The crucial components to capture in a chronicle are children's dialogue and interactions with one another, adults, the materials in use, and the ecosystem.

Chronicling allows you to bring the children's explorations and learning to life, inspiring a sense of purpose and dedication. It tells the story of each child's discoveries, connections, and experiences, showcasing the impact of your work. It makes children's growth and thinking process visible, affirming the importance of your role. Chronicles validate your work as an early childhood educator by showing how the intentionality of the revisiting journeys heutagogy and purposeful classroom designs scaffold and enhance the development of the whole child.

You might begin your chronicling with a space or wall where children can hang their photos, drawings, and dictations. Always ask permission from the children to add observations, anecdotes, and quotes from conversations. The space is a living document that changes as the children add new representations of their ideas. It is a place where children and educators can gather to engage in meaningful conversations about the concepts they are investigating.

Chronicling is a collaborative process in which children and adults research, rethink, and reflect together. The chronicling process emerges from authentic co-researching by adults and children. The children decide what needs to be chronicled. They select the photos, drawings, and artifacts to include and help organize them. Often, children take the pictures and videos themselves. They choose the format that best captures a revisiting journey.

Adults observe and record the children's conversations, actions, and interactions through written notes, photos, videos, and audio recordings and organize them in a way that makes the process visible. These observations help educators recognize the pivoting points (revisiting, rethinking, reflecting, reimagining, rediscovering, redesigning, and redefining) and plan accordingly. Chronicles can serve as data or evidence for educators as they study each child's development. You may have many questions as you chronicle, and these questions will offer insights into your values as an educator and how the program structure should be organized for the next steps in the revisiting journey.

Chronicling in Practice

To discover the data that will guide your work, you need to establish an organizational process for planning and chronicling the revisiting journeys. Systems for observing and recording children's theories will be unique to your program, as every program has its own culture and nuances. However, here are some general guidelines that can support you in this pursuit:

- Account for both recording and supervision.
- Determine your documenting tool.
- Reflect.

Account for Both Recording and Supervision

Select a time of day when you are comfortable taking observation data. Many educators find that a great time for observation is during exploration time. Set aside ten minutes to observe and record the children. If you work in a team-teaching system, plan with your coteacher who will be recording data and who will be supervising the children. Clear communication is key. If you work alone, select a time when the children are engaged in the various interest centers in your classroom. Select one area that is particularly busy so you can be present for supervision while also being able to record children's theories. If you are still working on your comfort and skill at chronicling while scanning and supervising the classroom, you could place a digital device in the classroom and record video for a short portion of the day—ideally ten to twenty minutes—so reviewing the video will not be a daunting task. Instead, reviewing the video will feel like watching a short film that offers intriguing insights into the children's ideas.

Determine Your Documenting Tool

Experiment with different types of tools for recording the children's theories. Test using notes (handwritten or entered directly into a digital device), videos, photos, and audio recordings. Determine which system works best for you. It may be a combination of all of them.

Reflect

Reflect at the end of the day with the children. Tell the children what you noticed. Ask them clarifying questions. Describe the theories you *think* they are testing. Gain insight directly from them. This collaborative reflection helps you determine your next steps in curriculum planning and encourages critical thinking in the children. Reflection is a muscle that needs to be exercised. When you reflect with the children, you are helping them develop this skill.

After reflecting with the children, practice your own reflection once all the children have been picked up by their families. You can reflect formally by brainstorming your own ideas for the next day, sharing your insights with colleagues to discover different perspectives, or seeking out support from supervisors and coaches about which path to take next. You can also reflect informally, such as on your commute home from work. Ask yourself the following questions:

- "What did the children test today?"
- "What did the children want to know today?"
- "What did the children discover today?"
- "What theories did I notice emerging?"
- "What unscripted materials might I be able to give the children tomorrow to support this journey?"

Answering these questions will support you in planning your next steps. They will help you organize your ideas. As you determine the theory that children are investigating, you can consider how you will embark on your parallel journey to plan for children's revisiting journeys.

Reflective Questions

- What strategies and systems could you use to capture and chronicle the children's play?
- Who could support you in this process?
- How can you encourage children to take the lead in the chronicling process?

Chronicling needs to be performed regularly and must be tailored to the children and their families. Tailoring happens when children take a leading role in the chronicling process. Each program can adapt the chronicles to best meet its structure and requirements. The following are some possible methods for chronicling revisiting journeys.

- chronicle walls
- collaborative portfolios
- storyboards with video

A **chronicle wall** is a space in the classroom where children can add their photos and drawings, recording the story of their journeys. Educators and children often review the chronicles on the wall to add to it, edit it, and ensure the story is visible and complete.

A **collaborative portfolio** could be a digital or printed portfolio. Like a chronicle wall, a portfolio is the collaborative work of educators and children, and the children are an integral part of the process as they help select the images and works to include in the portfolio. Establish a system by which you can digitally store photos, videos, and transcribed audio recordings in an organized fashion so you can look back at children's journeys in a meaningful and intentional way throughout the year. Multiple computer applications are available to help you organize and share their journeys digitally. You can also create printed portfolios that are available in your classroom for ongoing review. Children can pull a printed portfolio off the shelf and remind one another of the story that evolved in the revisiting journey.

You can organize a collaborative portfolio by children's journeys, with a separate section demonstrating each journey. For example, you might have a section about a journey into technology that features the children's story with their photos and words as they explored how to create and use their own tools. You can add sections to the portfolio over the year, allowing children to revisit their journeys and gain inspiration

for new twists and turns. At year's end, the portfolio is a testament to the learning, development, and growth that happened.

A **storyboard** guides the planning and editing of a final **video** that you create and screen at the end of a revisiting journey. Discuss the sequence and steps you need to take before you record a video using index cards, children's drawings, or photographs. Alongside the children, consistently reflect on how the process steers and changes the storyboard.

Keeping chronicles accessible in the classroom and giving children ownership of them can scaffold and support their revisiting journeys. It also gives children the chance to retell and share their journeys with their peers, sparking opportunities for collaboration. Access to chronicles empowers children to share their thoughts and assign meaning to their actions, behaviors, and play scenarios.

Following is an observation of how Jamal and Ari entered a revisiting journey of metacognition through sharing and revisiting their collaborative classroom portfolios and chronicles.

> The children have binders that serve as their portfolios in the classroom. Each binder is filled with chronicles personalized to the child and includes the observed journeys the children have taken. The portfolios contain photos, conversations, and narration to explain context and development. The children are vital in creating the portfolios. They can add a new idea or include a photo of a drawing

they think represents their thinking. They often come to the educators and ask to add a photo or a drawing to their portfolio.

The binders are kept on their own shelf in the classroom near the cozy space. The cozy space has comfortable child-sized cushioned chairs, a soft rug, a bookcase, and adult-sized seating so educators and families can comfortably sit and peruse books with the children throughout the day. We placed the portfolios here so the children would have a quiet space to collect and share their thoughts. We also thought about placing them so that each child could easily find their own binder. We discussed various ideas as a team, such as placing them in baskets, putting them in the bookcase, and so forth. Ultimately, we decided to put them on their own cubby shelf. This provides a clearly defined space so the children know where to find their binder and where to put it back when they are done.

The children frequently visit this space; Ari in particular keeps coming back to view the chronicles. He takes his binder and peers' binders off the shelf to look at and "read." There are times when Ari and Jamal share stories with one another, including what they were doing (their actions and behaviors) and why they were doing it (the reasoning and meaning they assigned to their play journeys). As they share stories, the children think and communicate about their own thinking. They are refining the tools and skills needed for reflection.

The children also enjoy adding materials to their own binders. They place in their binders the printed photos and documentation that their educators and families create and share. They also like to select artifacts, drawings, paintings, and written "stories" to keep in their binders. This sense of ownership empowers the children to take initiative in their own learning journeys.

Reflective Questions

- **Reflecting upon your program and all its nuances, how would you implement a system for the children to visit their portfolios?**
- **What strategies would you use to encourage the children to visit the portfolios?**
- **What factors, such as design space and daily schedule, could influence your implementation?**
- **How would visiting their portfolios support and enhance the whole development of the children in your program?**
- **What journeys do you see occurring while the children read and share their portfolios with one another?**

Making the Educator's Role Visible to Families

An essential part of chronicling a revisiting journey is making the educator's role visible. We encourage you as an educator to include your own learning in the revisiting journey chronicle. When you make your role visible, it allows you to reimagine yourself as an educator and embrace a dynamic process that invites you to research and continuously spark your creativity. Jessie's experience of chronicling revisiting journeys is a testament to how embracing a parallel journey can help educators overcome challenges and enhance their teaching practices. In bringing the stories of revisiting journeys to life, she shares with families, administrators, and colleagues all the learning that is taking place.

Parallel Journey

Jessie shares:

Our staff share a common desire to show the importance of the work that occurs at our school. We want families to understand how the children's revisiting journeys inform our planning to support the development of each child. As an administrator, I recognize the importance of creating a collaborative parallel journey with the educators to accomplish this together. We tested many different chronicling methods to see what would work best for us. Each educator had a unique style for chronicling the children's journeys. Some took notes in a notebook, some used clipboards strategically placed throughout the classroom, some used video recording, and some used audio recording. Communication and collaboration were critical to each educator's success in this process. They engaged in parallel journeys, shared their struggles, and brainstormed ideas and strategies together.

In our program, each classroom has two educators. We determined that for twenty minutes each day, one educator would be responsible for maintaining the safety and supervision of the group of children while the other educator recorded and chronicled the children's revisiting journeys. To support one another and maintain consistency and engagement, we brought these observations to weekly meetings to strategize, plan, review, amend, redesign, and reimagine our curriculum and environment to allow time and space for the children to extend and dive deeper into these journeys. By breaking the process into smaller steps, we accomplished our goals without becoming overwhelmed.

Each week the educators shared the stories of the revisiting journeys in an electronic format to give families easy access. By sharing stories this way, we gave families an opportunity to revisit the journeys at home with their children. The children can then share their stories and insights with the families, strengthening the relationship and connection between home and school. The chronicles included the parallel journeys educators took to support children, thus offering families a view of educators' interests and their commitment to seeing each child's unique strengths.

Reflective Questions

- How does the parallel journey process help families see educators' and children's work?
- How do parallel journeys deepen your own teaching practice and understanding of how young children develop and make meaning of the world?
- What captures your curiosity?

Sharing the individual portfolios with each child's family is a vital step in supporting children's revisiting journeys. Families learn why each journey is important and how the children's learning and development has been enhanced. Sharing portfolios also provides a pathway for collaboration with families. You can include the families in your study and research by encouraging them to share the journeys they observe at home. We recommend providing families with many options for participating, such as sharing photos the children take outside of school with a quick synopsis of what is occurring. This sharing creates a partnership with families that is meaningful and authentic and rooted in trust and collaboration.

Incorporating families into the chronicling process adds depth to the journeys children take. It helps children connect the home and school environments. As an educator, you can enhance and guide the journeys by incorporating into your plans the information families share with you about their home environments. You can redesign spaces to use materials and ideas from children's homes. You can also share with the families how the information they provided to you positively impacted their children's development and experiences while at school—another opportunity to help families understand and see the value of play and their children's revisiting journeys. Providing tangible evidence that families can see for themselves reinforces your assertions about their children's strengths and connections in the school setting.

Reflective Questions

- How will you create and structure the children's developmental portfolios using the revisiting journeys framework?
- What steps must you take to create and maintain the children's portfolios?
- What potential obstacles do you see in creating and maintaining the children's portfolios?
- How will you partner with families to share and deepen the experience of their children's portfolios?
- How will you use the individual portfolios to support the assessments you share with families about their children's observable learning and development in the context of revisiting journeys?

Organizing, writing chronicles, and guiding the revisiting process requires intentional work and flexibility. As an educator, you must work purposefully as you document and research the children's strengths, interests, actions, and interactions. You can change your classroom ecosystems with careful observation and reflection to magnify and extend the children's revisiting process. Collaboration with colleagues, families, and the children themselves will assist you in your efforts to provide an ecosystem that celebrates children's unique play and learning journeys as they grow and change during the year. In reframing how you view children's journeys, you support the whole child's development.

In the upcoming chapters, we are thrilled to share the unique and inspiring revisiting journeys of the children in our care. We also invited programs that actively participate in revisiting journeys with young children to share those journeys. We are deeply honored that the following programs agreed to share their knowledge, experience, and vision with us: Kinderoo Children's Academy (Ocala, Florida), Boulder Journey School (Boulder, Colorado), and William Paterson University Child Development Center (Wayne, New Jersey). Their diverse locations, languages, abilities, demographics, and combination of public and private programs, including kindergarten, make their contributions invaluable. We deeply respect and appreciate their commitment.

We hope that these revisiting journeys, which demonstrate a collaborative, reflective practice, will both delight and inspire you. Though the formats for the revisiting journeys are similar, each story is unique and represents the cultures of the children and educators of the program. In some cases, we have changed names to preserve confidentiality.

A revisiting journey is often messy. The story may not seem organized or easy to follow. It usually takes turns and detours as educators follow different pivoting points. Sometimes a small group of children decides to follow a different path led by their curiosity. Other times an entire group of children, along with the educators, engage in a revisiting journey together. Read the stories and follow the photographs; they will give you a clear overall picture of the children's revisiting journeys.

Each chapter that follows highlights the parallel journeys educators embarked on to support the children's inquiries. These parallel journeys are not just a part of the process—they are integral to it. By engaging in parallel journeys, educators can see their learning processes and practices as they implement the revisiting journey framework in their programs. Recognizing the educators' role in the process is crucial; we want you to feel valued and integral to the journey. Some parallel journeys demonstrate a collaborative, reflective practice, fostering a sense of community among educators. Others are written in the first person to show how journaling becomes part of the parallel journey process. Some revisiting journeys include photograph captions while others do not. We intentionally respect the program's stories as they were shared with us.

Organization of the Chapters

Each chapter includes boxes outlining the educators' parallel journeys. We believe that the parallel journey is an essential part of educators' work that needs to be made visible. At the end of each chapter, we include a box with reflective questions to deepen your understanding of the revisiting journey framework.

The following four chapters are stories from an early childhood program where Jessie served as director and educator. The pedagogy was inspired by the Loris Malaguzzi philosophy, in which educators and children coconstruct learning through hands-on experiences. These stories are based on the documented experiences of the children and educators at this program. We have changed the names to respect the privacy and dignity of all involved.

Chapters 10–13 are stories from early childhood programs across the United States who were willing to share the journeys their children and educators engaged in over time.

CHAPTER 6

Learning Through Inductive Reasoning

A Journey into Color Theory

This chapter focuses on how children learn through inductive reasoning. In this revisiting journey, children made decisions, discerned, predicted, and theorized. As the children mixed colors, they collected data based on their experiences and previous knowledge and then integrated the information to develop hypotheses. They tested their ideas to confirm whether their hypotheses were valid. Educators chronicled the journey and kept track of the children's theories. Each theory generated by the children was written down for further testing and investigation during the journey.

This chapter emphasizes the educators' parallel journeys as researchers. Parallel journeys are vital to the revisiting experience. They allow educators to make their learning visible. This chapter highlights how we took a proactive approach at the beginning of the school year to learning about color theory, the psychology of color, and how children perceive color. We used action research to guide the children. We observed, listened, and collected data that helped us define, design, and discover the next steps in the revisiting journey. Our parallel journeys as educators empowered us to deepen our curiosity and stay ahead of the questions children asked. We wanted to be prepared to respond to the various journeys children would lead us on as they explored color theory in detail. Each new pivoting point invited us to reflect on and rethink how we responded to the children's interests. We observed and listened to their comments and intentionally provoked and challenged their thinking.

Throughout the revisiting journey, we shared with the children our own parallel journeys. We wanted them to know that we were learning along with them. This approach helped build trusting relationships and let the children know that we value their thinking and ideas.

The Color Mixing Begins

This revisiting journey started at the beginning of the year. The ecosystem was designed simply, to let children change spaces as they gained knowledge and experience. In this case, we set an exploration to mix colors. From previous experience, we knew that children's learning is often guided by inductive reasoning, a process that encourages them to explore and discover. The invitation was simple yet engaging.

At the beginning of the new school year, we met with families to gather information about the children joining the group. We wanted to be prepared to support each child's individual strengths. Kia was an observant and perceptive child. She often watched what her peers did before engaging in play. Aaliyah was inclusive of all children and often negotiated to have everyone involved in play. We noticed that Aurelio was creative and engaged in play with all his senses. We discovered that Emma, while keen to observe, was not ready to actively engage with and touch paint and other sensory materials that might leave her hands "messy," prompting us to provide tools such as mixing sticks and gloves. Olivia was a natural leader who wanted other children to follow her lead. We noticed that Luna was creative and engaged with all her senses. Like Emma, she was not ready to touch paint or other sensory materials.

Designing an Invitation to Explore Color

Parallel Journey

At the beginning of the year, we educators came together to reflect on the temperaments, personalities, and learning dispositions of the children in our program. We discussed the unique support each child would require throughout the year. Then we designed the play ecosystem to intentionally enhance the children's engagement.

From experience, we knew that embarking on a journey into color theory would be fascinating for the children while also igniting our passion as educators. Observing the children's interest in the colors they selected and how they mixed new colors would provide ample opportunities to understand their dispositions and approaches to learning while we built strong relationships with them. The parallel journey not only provides an effective way to collect the information needed for compliance but also gives us a methodology to define who the children in the program are, to design the ecosystem to support children's interests, and to discover the data that will enhance children's learning.

We discussed the strategies we would use to collect data and how we would manage the different paths the revisiting journey would take us. To prepare for the research, we discussed how we would chronicle the children's journey and what strategies we would employ to ensure we documented all the children's ideas and theories. We also talked about implementing action research. This collaborative process requires educators to collect data that may require immediate action to respond to children's theories. Parallel journeys are integral to action research. We spent time analyzing each part of the action research process to create a system that worked for us.

With much reflection, we decided to refocus our attention on supporting children's inquiry and not just collecting data to write compliance reports. This was a liberating moment that led to designing a robust approach to the revisiting journeys. We discussed our individual and collective commitment to our practices. We challenged one another with critical questions. We supported one another by acknowledging that we might be in disequilibrium as we explored new ideas and challenged our existing assumptions. We also recognized that we might need extra support to give meaning to our learning.

We recognized that we all valued collaboration with one another, the families, and the children. However, we all gave different meanings to collaboration. We spent time discussing what collaboration meant and how we would create a collaborative approach. We agreed that we would meet regularly to revisit our goals, and we based the collaborative process on the goals we established. This was comforting because we knew we could come back and revisit our practices without judgment. We knew we all had different understandings of what it means to teach and educate children. We gave ourselves permission to reflect, redesign, and reconstruct our practices as we integrated new information we discovered in our observations.

We acknowledged that we don't always have all the information on a given topic. Instead, we made a commitment to spend time researching before answering children's questions, both with the children and on our own.

Translating our reflections into action, we created a flexible plan to guide our parallel journeys. Since it was the beginning of the year, we focused our attention on getting to know the children. We started a strengths journal for every child. We supported one another as we learned not to focus on deficits. This helped us shift our thinking about children and supported us in noticing our biases and perceptions.

To increase collaboration with the children, we created a chronicle wall to tell the story of the revisiting journeys. We decided that the children would be integral contributors to the chronicle wall. We decided that we educators needed time each week to reflect, rethink, reconstruct, and redesign together. The schedule was shifted to accommodate for this valuable time.

We set up the color-mixing exploration in the outdoor art studio. The children enjoyed spending time outside, so putting the exploration outside allowed us to make it part of the daily play. We set the space to draw the children in. We set out clear pump bottles with the primary colors, small containers, and a variety of mixing sticks and brushes for children to independently select the colors they wanted to mix.

Children could use mason jars to save the colors they created. Wooden boxes held the jars with paintbrushes, adding dimension to the provocation to make the space eye-catching and interesting to the children. We wanted to prompt their curiosity while supporting their lines of inquiry.

The first children to join this space were Ari, Ella, Aaliyah, and Olivia. They carefully mixed the primary colors and commented on what they discovered. They realized that mixing blue and yellow created green. They talked among themselves, and they asked questions that prompted further mixing. They added red to green, thinking that it would make a different shade of green. They experimented with smaller quantities of blue and yellow to see how many colors of green they could mix. Olivia picked up her mixing jar and compared it to various leaves in the environment. She exclaimed, "I can only make some of the greens but not all greens." Ella then started mixing the colors to create different greens.

The children labeled the colors as they mixed them. This allowed children to feel ownership over their colors. On each label, we wrote the color name and amount of the colors used so that children could revisit and re-create them as needed. They created the most remarkable names! Aurelio created the name Mifucius Pink, and Ella named her deep purple paint Sky Fly. Aaliyah, drawing inspiration from her friendship with Ella, named her paint Ella-Rock-Plate-Paloony. Diego named his paint Mommy, Daddy Purple. The children surprised us with their questions and how they predicted which primary colors produced which new colors when mixed.

Parallel Journey

We collected anecdotal data and took photos and videos of the children mixing the colors. We captured their theories and ideas through observation and documentation. We noted children's individual strengths both in their journals and on the chronicle walls. We shared the data in our weekly reflective gathering. We were all fascinated by how the children focused on creating the various colors and how they named them.

Exploring Primary, Secondary, and Tertiary Colors

After a few days of experimenting with primary colors, the children's questions sparked a new phase in the revisiting journey as they began trying to match colors with objects in the classroom ecosystem. The children started mixing secondary colors and realized that new colors emerged. This encouraged them to mix the secondary colors to create tertiary colors. As educators, we saw this as an opportunity to plan the next steps in challenging the children's understanding of color theory. We were inspired by their curiosity and knew it was time to engage in our parallel journey.

Parallel Journey

We noticed that Ari, Ella, Aaliyah, and Olivia had begun to mix the secondary colors. We wanted to support them in their exploration and next invite them to mix the secondary colors to create a tertiary set of colors. We also continued to provide the original exploration for children still engaged in mixing primary colors.

Jessie volunteered to learn more about how colors are created. We explored mixing ourselves and we learned how to use the color wheel. We learned that the terms *hue*, *color*, *tint*, and *shade* have different meanings. We realized that we had been using them interchangeably, so going forward we wanted to give children the correct terminology.

We wanted to deepen our understanding of color theory. We recognize that the more we know about a topic, the more equipped we are to research and learn along with the children. We focused on the work of Josef Albers (1888–1976) and his extensive explorations of color. Albers and his wife, Anni Albers, were pioneering twentieth-century artists whose work transformed the way people see color and how we make art. We were fascinated by his book *Interaction of Color*, which is considered a masterwork in art education. The principles presented in the book serve as a guide to the exploration of color theory. What intrigued us the most was Josef Albers's explanation that colors can only be understood in relation to other colors. This means that how someone perceives a color can change depending on the colors that surround it. Albers argues that the way to learn about color is through experience and by trial and error.

After reading Albers's book *Homage to the Square*, in which he uses only one or two colors to create contrast, we decided to invite children to explore two colors at a time. We started using black and white in juxtaposition to light blue. We wanted children to experience how colors create harmony when they are juxtaposed.

We also prepared a list of reflective questions to use with the children as we revisited the color mixings of the day:

- What happens when you add more of one color to another color?
- What do you notice about the colors after you mix them?
- What colors look good with other colors?

- What other colors can you create? What do you need to create them?
- What color combinations can you put together? Can you replicate colors from nature?

Teaching is about asking the right questions. We can't anticipate exactly which questions to ask, but we can practice formulating questions to be ready to guide children into inquiry.

As the children continued to mix, create, and name colors, they started to talk about how they could make the colors "soft." Ella asked, "I want light blue. How do I make light blue?"

Parallel Journey

We met to reflect on the children's experience. We decided that the children were getting comfortable with mixing colors, so it was time to introduce white and black paint to explore tints and shades. We wanted to eventually explore how brightness saturated the original hues to create different tints. We agreed to wait until the children made connections and started to ask questions about lighter and darker colors.

Before introducing white and black paint to the children, we educators experimented with mixing white paint into the colors we had created. We kept a chart and tabulated what happened. We wanted to share our experience with the children. As we mixed white with other colors, we noticed we were creating pastels. We learned by trial and error that we had to begin with white and then add the other colors gradually. We researched the reasons to start with white and learned that starting with white allows for a more precise and gradual process of adding color.

Exploring White Paint to Create Tints

As the children continued to mix the primary colors, Jessie invited them to join her in a small group gathering. Jessie showed them how mixing white with blue creates a tint. She asked the children: "What do you think: Should we add white to the blue paint, or add blue to the white paint?" Immediately Ella started adding blue to the white paint in her jar. She shared with her peers that she was going to create the sky. She took the blue paint pump and began vigorously pumping it into her jar.

Looking at the sky above them, Ari stated, "You need to use white for the clouds." He passed Ella the white paint pump jar for her to use.

As she added the white paint, Ella shared, "When I swirl it, there's little lines in it."

Aaliyah jumped up from her seat at the studio and raced over to look in Ella's jar. She exclaimed, "It's different!" She then returned to her spot, grabbed her own jar of blue paint, and stated, "I don't have any swirls in mine."

Olivia said, "You can add white and make them."

Aaliyah asked, "Can I have it?"

Ella said, "When I'm done."

Aaliyah then stood next to Ella counting the number of white paint pumps she added to her jar. Rather than mixing her paint with a paintbrush, Ella put the lid on top of the jar and began shaking it up and down.

Ari asked, "Why are you doing that?"

Olivia said, "You're going to break it."

Ella continued to shake the jar up and down, staring only at her jar. After a few more shakes, she exclaimed, "There!" and placed the jar back down on the table. She carefully opened the lid. She told her peers, "Look! I made the sky! My blue is lighter, and I see all the white. There are the clouds. This white has to stay a little separate like those clouds over there."

The children continued to mix various shades of blue, drawing inspiration from peers' clothing, their own imaginations, and their own hypotheses. Ari wanted to discover if he could turn his blue paint completely into white. This helped us reflect on the different ways we could revisit color theory with the children.

Adding Red Paint

During a group gathering, we introduced the term *achromatic*, or having no hue (color). We started with white paint and added a few drops of red paint. As we mixed the paint, we told the children that white is achromatic. Since the children had already been exploring mixing white paint, we were curious as to how they would share their knowledge with one another and what connections they would make to the concept of tint. Educator Jessie asked how many shades of red tint they thought we could create. All at once the children started saying different numbers.

Olivia said, "I can make millions, millions."

Noah added, "I can make more and more."

Using this exciting moment, we suggested we tally the number of red tints the children created. We moved an easel close to the outdoor art studio for children to test and tally the colors they created.

We kept the primary color mixing in the outdoor studio for children to revisit and made white paint available. We also set a new invitation with red paint and color-mixing plates. We wanted the children to notice the different tints they were creating. We hoped to challenge the children to see how red and white can become pink, not just tints of red. A friendly competition began as they challenged one another with new theories about the color tints they could create.

Ari said, "I can make this many," and he lifted five fingers.

Diego joined in the conversation, saying, "I can make as many as the circles on the plate."

We noticed that Elias loved to mix and create paint. However, he had no desire to use the paints he mixed. Instead, he offered to mix paints for peers.

The children eagerly encouraged one another to add more or less white paint to the different colors. After adding more red to the white paint, the children began to notice the color pink emerging.

Emma observed, "Wait, look! It is pink; you made pink," as she pointed to Aurelio's color-mixing plate.

Educator Jessie asked, "Is pink a red tint, or is it a different color?" Before giving children the answer, we listened to their hypotheses.

Malacki said, "It is red tint because it has red."

Jovani argued, "It is just pink because it matches my shirt, and my shirt is pink."

Santiago added, "It is both because you use both when you paint."

As children mixed white paint, they started to question how they could make a color darker. This told us that it was time to introduce black paint.

Introducing Black Paint to Create Shades

Parallel Journey

Before we moved forward, we needed to rediscover and rethink the information in our observations and data. We carefully reviewed the chronicles to determine if there were any gaps in the children's theories. We asked ourselves if the children had all the information they needed to test their hypotheses. We discussed the changes we needed to make to encourage children to explore color mixing further.

We realized that we had not yet introduced black paint. To rectify this, during our educators' gathering we researched how to introduce black paint to the children. This led us to the understanding that adding black to color paint creates shades. A shade is a mixture of a pure color (primary, secondary, or tertiary) and black. Black darkens the color, but the hue remains the same.

We decided that we would introduce mixing black during a group gathering. We thought that engaging in a discussion of shade would deepen children's understanding of the complexity of color.

We gathered the children in the outdoor studio, where we introduced black paint and explained how adding black to any color creates shades of that color. We placed black paint in a container and added a few drops of red paint. At first the children thought that mixing red into the black paint would make pink. They had made a connection to the way that white and red make pink. We then added red paint to a different container, and using an eyedropper, we added a few drops of black paint.

Ari said, "Black is like night, dark."

Diego followed Ari's thinking and added, "If we put too much black, it will just be dark."

Liam joined in the conversation, "Black paint is different than white paint."

The children concluded that black paint had to be added to other color paints, rather than adding a color into black paint.

We added black to the color exploration. After a few minutes of mixing colors with black paint themselves, the children noticed that the red paint only got darker when mixed with black, rather than turning pink as it had when mixed with white. New questions emerged. As educators,

we were happy that we had spent time researching ahead of the children's explorations.

Educator Jessie invited the children to research too. The children decided to ask, "Is pink a color or a shade of red tint?" The question itself is confusing because a shade is a darker hue (color + black), while a tint is a lighter hue (color + white). However, it is important to follow the questions children generate and be flexible as they find answers.

Olivia said, "Google it. That is what my mommy do."

Educator Jessie looked up the question online. The first answer we found was as follows: "Pink is a tint of the primary color red, so it is not on a traditional color wheel. It is made by mixing white and red together, creating a paler version of red. On modern color wheels, pink is viewed alongside red and mauve."

The children became curious about shades, considering whether they were different colors or a hue of the same color. Ari prompted a conversation about what the color black is. He shared his theory that adding black to other colors impacts their shades and tints. We documented each hypothesis to keep track of them.

Diego asked, "Is dark red a new color?"

Olivia, always first to respond, said, "It is just dark red because we added black paint."

Parallel Journey

We gathered at the end of the week to share data and discover the children's stories. The data we collected guided us to redefine what we knew about the children and to redesign the color-mixing invitation to add complexity to the children's thinking. We reviewed the theory card to make connections that would give us insight into their thinking. We decided that the children needed to constantly revisit color theory and that when their hypotheses did not produce the expected results, they needed time to revisit and reconstruct the mixing process and revisit their theory. We discussed strategies to guide children to carefully record the amount of paint they use. We created color journals for the children to record their color-mixing discoveries. Of course, children often scribbled beside the smudges of color, which is developmentally appropriate before children can form letters. Families often came into the program to help the children dictate the observations, and they wrote the children's words in their journals. The purpose of the journals was to validate and preserve their work, not to assess their writing ability.

The Color Wheel

Parallel Journey

Since the children had been mixing color for a while, we thought it was time to introduce the color wheel and how to use it. During our weekly reflective

meeting, Jessie was curious about how the color wheel helps artists use color. She shared that during her research she found historical information explaining how the color wheel was created. This led us down rabbit trails as we each researched the value of the color wheel.

However, we knew that we had to simplify the information for the children. We decided just to introduce them to the basics, and we were prepared to go deeper with the children who showed interest. We decided to focus on the idea that color combinations bring harmony to art. Color harmony is the relationship between two colors that can create an aesthetic composition (a thoughtful arrangement of colors to create a visually harmonious design) when placed together.

We researched different types of color wheels and bought a few of them. We played with each of the color wheels, exploring the primary, secondary, and tertiary colors. The Cox color wheel provided a variety of colors in a spectrum. The C&T Publishing color wheel gave the name and numbers of the different colors. The Waldorf color wheel showed softer tints and shades. We also collected paint sample cards from the local hardware store.

At a group gathering, we invited the children to explore the various color wheels we'd purchased. The children identified that when they mix blue, yellow, and red, they can make many other colors. We talked about how red, blue, and yellow are primary colors. We asked the children if they had any theories about how the various colors in the color wheel could be created. We recorded these theories for the children to use as they continued to mix colors.

Each time the children created new secondary colors, we compared them to the color wheel. When the children looked at the C&T wheel, they decided to start numbering the colors they created. In collaboration with the children, we created a new color chart. We charted how many secondary colors were created by combining two colors, and the children named them and numbered them. Once the children mixed all the primary colors, we invited them to mix the secondary colors to create tertiary colors. The charting process continued. The children asked to add the black and white paint to create more colors.

The conversations were engaging, and we knew that children understood color theory because they noticed the degrees of hues and tints and developed a sharper eye. They started to be more selective with the colors they used in their art. Their descriptions of the colors they created became more complex. They used color theory terminology as they described their art and when they mixed new colors as they needed them.

Ari said, "I'm making orange because I like orange. We have an orange tree in our backyard. It doesn't have any oranges on it right now."

Elias added, "Mine looks like it's green. Look!" He then lowered the jar to show Ari what was inside.

Ari said, "You need more yellow. It looks blue to me." He then picked up the yellow paint pump. "Do you want me to do it?"

Elias continued to hold his jar out to Ari and nodded. Ari began pumping more yellow paint into Elias's jar.

Ella proclaimed, "I wanna make a rainbow!" She began adding all three colors of paint into her jar.

Olivia, busy mixing her own paint of red and white, stated, "You can't make a rainbow like that. It makes brown." Ella responded, "I'm making a rainbow." She continued to stir all three colors together in her jar. After a few moments, she looked at her jar. The paints mixed to form a brown hue. She proudly held the jar up and said, "I maked a brown rainbow!"

Olivia looked up from her mixing and added, "I wanna make a brown rainbow too!" After mixing their "brown rainbows," both Ella and Olivia created paintings of rainbows using their brown paint.

To deepen children's thinking, we introduced the board book *Pantone Colors*. This book introduces children to nine basic colors and twenty shades created from the nine original colors. We added paint swatches so the children could compare and contrast the colors. The children predicted which color

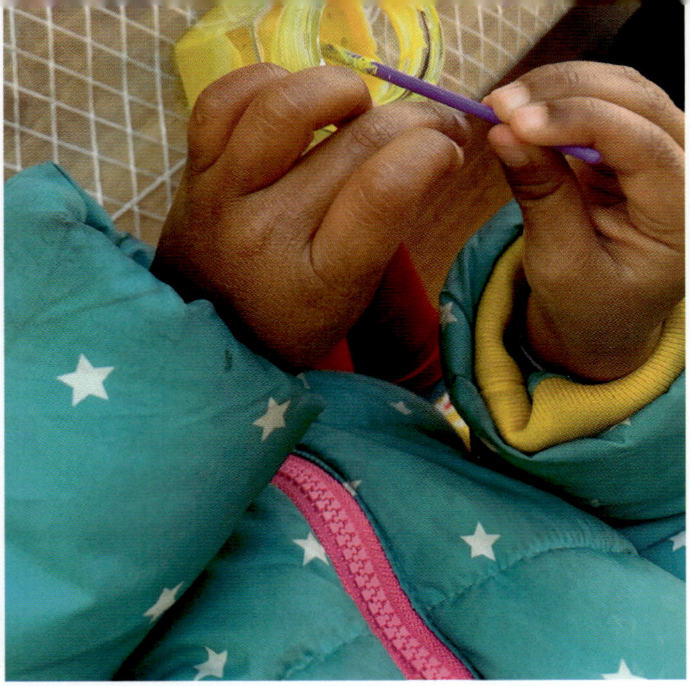

would result from mixing two together. Then together they started mixing colors to match the swatches.

The children began to use the paint they mixed and labeled in their art projects. They no longer asked for the pink paint. They had learned they could mix red with white to create different shades of pink. They began to talk about colors with passion, describing how various colors achieve different effects in their paintings. They described how they felt as they mixed each color. We could see that they were beginning to understand color theory because they were using the vocabulary.

Jamal, who enjoyed learning how things work, exclaimed, "Red is a primary color, but white is not!"

Ari, the master negotiator, offered, "White is no color. It is chromanin," referring to the fact that white is achromatic and has no shade.

Revisiting Black Paint

At this point, we reintroduced black paint. We wanted the children to understand that black is not technically a color, but is rather the absence of light or color. We invited the children to mix black paint with blue paint using eyedroppers. We showed them how to start with the blue paint and add a few drops of black at a time. We wanted to see whether they would notice that black can be used to create contrast and enhance other colors. We listened to their comments and descriptions as they mixed the paint.

Kia exclaimed, "Look, I made purple!" then continued to test various shades and purple hues.

Diego, Aurelio, Liam, and Olivia made connections between brightness and white and between darkness and black. They searched for items that were white and black. They wanted objects they could use to test their idea of what makes color brighter. They started placing items on our light table. Educator Jessie brought out the overhead projector to further explore light and color. The children discussed how black is dark and how white is light. They used different transparent and opaque items as they tested new color combinations.

In the meantime, we set an invitation for the children to compare and contrast how colors change when we add white and black. The children used the paint swatches and the color wheel to predict how much white or how much black paint they needed to achieve different tints and shades.

A few days into the exploration of black, Ari, who enjoys discovering the "why" behind things, asked, "If black is dark of color, is white the light in color?" He prompted a conversation about what the color black is and how adding it to other colors impacts their shades and tints, posing reasons and theories to support his many hypotheses. It was obvious that he enjoyed the scientific method.

Parallel Journey

Hearing children describe their ideas and reconstruct their thinking is always heartwarming. The children's continued interest in mixing paint kept us engaged and invested in their learning journey. We noticed that spending

time exploring colors gave them a new set of vocabulary words.

Our continuing research into color theory took us to the website of the Smithsonian Institution, where we learned that the English physicist Sir Isaac Newton experimented with prisms and discovered that clear white light was composed of seven different visible colors. Since we knew that Kai enters inquiry through history, we thought this information was important to share with the children.

We thought it was fascinating how some people believe that white is the "sum of all colors," a misconception that arises from the assumption that the only colors that exist are those within the light spectrum. If this were true, we wouldn't have the colors brown and magenta. On the other hand, there's the idea that black is "the absence of color." Considering these ideas opened up a world of questions we could pose to the children, inviting them to explore and share their hypotheses and actively participate in the learning process.

- Is color only what appears in the light spectrum?
- What colors exist outside of the light spectrum?
- Are black and white also colors?

We wondered how to invite children to explore light (white) and the absence of light (black) beyond color paints. We knew it was essential to pause and rethink what we knew and how we would challenge children to explore new perspectives before they redesigned their ideas. We gathered one evening to relax and test our theories and ideas. We played with the tools and materials we would introduce to the children, enjoying the process. We experimented with the light table, overhead projector, and outdoors using different natural lights. We explored opacity, transparency, projection, and reflection and their impact on color. We wanted to ensure that children would make connections to the absence of light as well as the intensity of light.

As the children began testing ideas about lights and shadows and began spending less time color mixing, we realized that the revelations about black and white were a pivoting point in the revisiting journey. It was time to explore color theory through lights and shadows, putting aside the paint. We were excited to see where this new journey would take us.

Reflective Questions

- How do you identify a revisiting journey?
- What information and knowledge do you need to support children's revisiting journeys?
- What evidence do you need to determine when multiple revisiting journeys are emerging?
- What plans do you have in place to support children as they pivot in the revisiting journey?
- How often do you need to gather to discover the information from the data you collect?
- What evidence do you need to know that a pivoting point has emerged?

MAKE
INK
Golden
Rod

CHAPTER 7

Learning Through Scientific Thinking

A Journey into Natural Ink Making

In this chapter, the educators supported the children's exploration of art as they made inks from a variety of natural herbs, spices, and pigments. The educators embarked on their own parallel journey, actively learning techniques and strategies for ink making. In the process, they acquired basic principles of scientific thinking that they could share with the children. These parallel journeys helped educators organize their thoughts effectively as they guided children in their exploration.

How Flowers Get Their Color

During our daily walks in late spring or early summer, the jacaranda trees are in the peak of blooming (in our area jacaranda trees bloom twice a year, in late spring and again in early summer). The beautiful shades of blue and deep purple create a mesmerizing landscape in our neighborhood. As the jacarandas shed their flowers, they leave a purple-blue stain on the sidewalk.

Some children noticed that the fallen flowers left colorful marks on the sidewalk.

They became curious, picked them up, and rubbed them to see the stain on their hands. They stepped on the petals, pounding them into the cement to see if the color would transfer.

Noah exclaimed, "Look, I am painting!" as he stomped on the flowers. The children had many questions and hypotheses about how the flowers left marks on the cement.

Rebecca, who loved to garden and liked to document the changes in the environment, shared her theory: "The flowers are blue because the rain makes them blue."

Kia softly asked, "We don't have a lot of rain, so how can the flowers still be blue?"

Always curious, Harper shared her hypothesis: "It kinda has a little paint when you walk on it."

We continued our walk and returned to the classroom for lunch and rest. Later in the afternoon, we found Emma sketching the jacaranda flowers in the outdoor art space. She was carefully mixing blue and white paint to approximate the purple-blue of the flowers. As she mixed, she described her sketches to Harper, who was sitting beside her. Harper posed what we all thought was an interesting question: "I wonder if the flowers can make paint."

Parallel Journey

As part of our ongoing practice, we often audio record, video record, or write down our conversations. We try to do it as often as we can. We have developed a keen ear and a strong listening pedagogy to know when the children have developed a theory. This is a skill that grows with time and consistency. As we looked over our observations and notes, we reconsidered the children's interesting theories about how the jacaranda flowers got their color.

Rebecca: "The flowers are blue because the rain makes them blue."

Harper: "We don't have a lot of rain, so how can the flowers still be blue?"

Emma: "I wonder if the flowers can make paint."

Noah: "Look, I am painting!"

Every theory was an invitation for us to research further. First, we wanted to understand the science behind how flowers release their color. We discovered that the natural pigments (anthocyanins, carotenoids, and flavonoids) found in the flower petals are released when the petals are crushed or soaked. The color created depends on the pigment. We also learned that we could affect the release of the pigment by adjusting pH levels with substances like lemon juice or baking soda. We realized that this revisiting journey would challenge us to constantly research the science behind what we were doing.

We were excited that Noah had participated in a group exploration. It was the first time he had made comments and shared his ideas. We wanted him to expand his social abilities and engage in more collaboration with other children. During a group gathering, we revisited the questions and theories the children had about how the flowers and leaves stained the sidewalk. We shared photos of our walk and revisited their ideas and new discoveries. As the children saw the photos and revisited their hypotheses, their curiosity was sparked again, and they were eager to learn more.

Parallel Journey

Before we present an exploration to the children, we test it and reflect on what works and what needs changing. We decided to start with flower pounding to transfer color onto cotton fabric or handmade paper. We thought that exploring the stains and marks left by the flowers could lead to greater understanding of how flowers get their color.

At our educators' reflective gathering, we pounded the flowers on both cotton fabric and handmade paper. We discovered that we needed to refine our choice of tools and materials. We started by using a mallet to pound directly on the flowers, but the color did not transfer. We tried using a rolling pin, but that did not work either. After a few attempts, we placed a piece of absorbent paper on top of the flowers. The paper absorbed the excess water from the flower, making the color more evident because it was not diluted by the liquid. Accordingly, we tried the handmade paper, and the color was more evident on the paper than on the cloth because of the paper's absorbing qualities. We also tested spraying both the fabric and handmade paper with baking soda mixed in water. The color was not as bright. We experimented and learned as we changed the process. We decided that mallets would be the best tool to introduce to the children, along with the cotton fabric and the handmade paper, so they could experiment on their own.

The chance to revisit our methods and rediscover more refined solutions is perhaps the most enjoyable part of our role as educators. This adaptability and resilience in problem solving is what empowers us and instills confidence in our abilities. We are not just teaching but also learning alongside the children.

Together we can reimagine a multitude of possibilities, fostering a sense of connection and teamwork.

During our walks, we invited the children to collect flowers and petals that had fallen from the trees. We introduced an invitation for children to pound the flowers onto both cotton fabric and handmade paper. We gathered in small groups to show them how to spray the fabric or handmade paper with water and baking soda. We gave children the option to place the flowers under the cotton fabric or the handmade paper and began gently pounding it with wooden mallets. We delighted in the children's comments as they watched the flowers stain the cotton fabric and handmade paper.

The children enjoyed the pounding. Jamal, who was very observant and always wanted to discover how things worked, said, "Can I try a real hammer?" He ran and brought a hammer from the tool area. We noticed how he shifted back and forth between pounding with the mallet and pounding with the hammer. He exclaimed, "The hammer makes more stain!"

Ari, ever the negotiator, said, "Jamal, let's try a rock and see what happens." Jamal and Ari ran to find rocks they could use for pounding. They noticed how the weight of the mallets and the rocks made a difference in the imprints. They counted how many times they had to pound to leave deeper stains.

We left the materials for children to revisit throughout the week. We were excited that the children continued to test their ideas using both the cotton fabric and the handmade paper.

Noah placed the paper on the floor and started stomping. He exclaimed excitedly, "See, I am painting!"

The children joined him and started stomping on the paper. Educator Jessie took a large piece of handmade paper and placed it on the floor. Noah took the spray bottle and made the paper wet. Other children placed flowers both on top of and under the paper. Together they counted, "One, two, three, jump." After seeing the results of their jumping,

the children decided that the mallets worked better to make flower imprints.

Exploring Water Absorption

Once again, the children provided us with the next steps in the revisiting journey. We decided to acknowledge Rebecca's hypothesis and give her the time to test her thinking: "The flowers are blue because the rain makes them blue."

Rebecca's question ignited our curiosity and initiated a collaborative research process. Together we delved into the concept of water absorption in plants, a process by which water is drawn up through the roots to all parts of the plant.

As we continued our research and contemplated the various ways to test Rebecca's hypothesis, the children engaged in their own experiments, testing methods to extract color from fresh flowers. We added coffee filters, tissue paper, straws, eyedroppers, and liquid watercolor to the outdoor art studio. Jovani mixed various liquid watercolors. He took a brush and dipped it into the water, then tested the color on a paper towel. He watched as the water was absorbed and spread, staining the paper towel. He yelled, "Come, see how water moves!" Jessie asked, "I wonder if this is the way water gets into the flowers?"

Parallel Journey

We continued to research and test water absorption to understand why the jacaranda flowers transferred so much water when we pounded them on homemade paper versus when we stomped on them on the sidewalk during our walk. We tested reusable acrylic straws, plastic syringes, and eyedroppers to see how water moved on absorbent paper such as coffee filters and napkins.

We wanted children to learn about capillary action so they could use the information to test their hypotheses. We researched the scientific process of capillary action. We learned that just as humans have veins and arteries that move blood around inside the body, plants have xylem to transport water from the roots upward to the rest of the plant.

We were particularly curious to see whether children would connect the movement of water in the straw and syringes to flowers absorbing water. We reminded ourselves that learning is not about finding the correct answer but about taking risks and formulating more questions.

We gathered the children and shared Jovani's discovery about what happened when he placed the wet brush on the paper towel. We also revisited Jessie's question: "I wonder if this is the way water gets into the flowers?"

We introduced the acrylic straws and plastic syringes and invited children to sip water from their cups with the straws. We wanted to see if they noticed how water moved through the straw. We demonstrated how they could place the straw inside the water and place their finger on the end of the straw to hold the water in place. Kamal, the performer, blew bubbles in the water. "Look, when I blow, I make bubbles."

Educator Jessie asked, "What happens when you suck on the straw?" Kamal answered, "I can drink the water." Educator Jessie added, "So the water can move up and down the straw. I wonder if the same happens when the flowers get their colors." The question brought the exploration back to the original revisiting journey.

Austin used the straw to drop water on a paper towel and exclaimed, "Look, the water is moving." Austin's discovery triggered a new set of questions, and Jessie invited children to observe and record in their journals how the color expanded as they dropped the liquid water color into the napkin. Jessie's curiosity led her to observe if the children made a connection to water absorption in plants, or if they would need further guidance and research.

We left the coffee filters set up and gave children plenty of time to revisit the exploration. Elias and Harper spent most of the outdoor time painting the filters. They first used the bright liquid watercolors. We observed Harper walking over to the faucet and

filling a cup with water. She tested the water on the coffee filter and exclaimed, "It is just wet." She then filled the eyedropper with red watercolor and dropped a few drops on the wet coffee filter. She quietly said, "It now looks soft red." She took another water filter, dropped red paint, and watched as the watercolor moved; she then dropped some water on the same coffee filter. As she tested each idea, she quietly talked through the process. She tested every color and used different quantities of water. After forty-five minutes, she exclaimed, "Flowers get color when we water them." We knew she had made the connection we were looking for! We invited her to share her findings with the other children. She shone with pride as she stood before the group to demonstrate how she tested the water and the paint moving on the paper.

Parallel Journey

To solidify our findings, we educators revisited the concept of capillary absorption and how flowers get their color. We were curious if there were other experiments we could introduce to the children to deepen their thinking about how flowers get their colors. We also wanted to introduce water measurement to the children. We learned about a flower experiment that uses food coloring to tint white flowers. We decided not to test the experiment ahead of time. Instead, we wanted to learn what would happen along with the children.

We purchased white carnations from the local flower shop and placed them in jars with water. We would introduce the experiment during a group gathering.

We invited the children to select food coloring to add to the water in the jars using the eyedroppers. We counted the number of drops they added to the water. We challenged the children during our morning meeting to discover and document in their journals the changes they observed. We also started a large chart to tabulate the results. The children visited the space throughout the day, noting how the carnations changed color.

Can Flowers Make Paint?

Our walks continued, and the children found more stains on the cement. As time passed, the weather got slightly cooler (although the weather in San Diego, California, does not change drastically). The jacaranda trees started to bloom again. This time, the flowers were light blue and yellow. The children noticed the change, and the conversation about making paint with flowers started again. We knew it was time to revisit Emma's question: "I wonder if the flowers can make paint."

This was a pivoting point in the revisiting journey, and we educators played a crucial role in addressing Emma's interest. She was an incredible artist, and throughout the pounding and water absorption explorations, we supported her in comparing the color imprints to the paint the class had mixed during the color wheel exploration. The children had many questions about how nature creates different colors. The children were particularly interested in Emma's question: "How did the flowers paint the floor?" Once again, the children's interest gave us a clue to reflect, revisit what we discovered, and redesign the next steps in the journey.

Parallel Journey

The children's inquisitive natures and their theories sparked our research into the use of natural pigments for creating paint and ink. Emma's intriguing question "I wonder if flowers make paint?" became a catalyst for our exploration. The children had already explored extracting the color of flowers and plants by pounding. They had also made connections with how flowers get their color from water and soil. We knew that they were ready to do more complex thinking.

We were curious to deepen our understanding of plant and color staining and explore how the pigments from flowers and other natural materials contribute to ink making. We delved into books and articles, discovering the art of making paint with natural pigments. Our research taught us that environmental factors, such as sun, rain, wind, and soil, are endlessly complex and constantly contribute to the colors of flowers and leaves. We learned that plants have tannins to protect them from fungi, bacteria, viruses, insects, and

other herbivorous animals that feed on them. Pollen from flowers can also make colorful pigments. Pollen and tannins are responsible for leaving behind the stains on the sidewalk that the children noticed. Rain and the morning dew rinse the tannins from the fallen flowers and foliage, leaving stains on the sidewalk, similar to how black tea leaves behind a tannin stain on porcelain cups.

We found the book *Make Ink: A Forager's Guide to Natural Inkmaking* by Jason Logan. When we read the book and explored the recipes, we realized that making natural ink with the children would be a great way to continue the color-mixing journey. We were also excited to explore natural processes with the children and help them connect meaningfully with nature. We were relieved to learn that making natural ink was simple. We could use any pigment-rich ingredient (flowers, leaves, or other naturally produced pigments) and boil them with vinegar and salt. Adding gum arabic would preserve the ink to be used over time.

Our goal was not to turn the exploration into a structured lesson about plants and flowers. Instead, we aimed to foster the children's autonomy and encourage them to develop their own hypotheses as they discovered new information. Their active role in the learning process was a key aspect of our approach.

We spent more time reflecting together and researching how flowers acquire their color. We learned that the color of the flowers comes from the concentration of pigments. We shared our experiences with food items that had stained our clothing, such as memories of agua de jamaica (hibiscus water) staining a white blouse. We also remembered that turmeric can leave yellow stains when it is not handled carefully. We compared turmeric to the yellow pollen left by lilies. The more we shared, the more excited we became about exploring making ink.

The more we learned, the more confusing things got, and the more questions emerged. We reminded ourselves to embrace a mindflex attitude (one that avoids rigidity and allows us to change as needed) and allow the flow of discovery to guide us. As part of the process, we encountered some unexpected discoveries that helped us make new connections.

For instance, we learned that fewer tannins in a plant produced less pigmentation, creating lighter colors in plants and flowers. The more tannins a plant has, the darker the pigmentation (color). This was interesting to us, because it is similar to how humans get their skin color. The more melanin a person has, the more pigmentation and the darker the skin. Less melanin and less pigmentation make the skin lighter. We wondered whether children would make this same connection. We made a note to investigate a connection between the color of flowers and human skin color and then revisit this concept with the children. We thought a new revisiting journey might emerge.

Making Ink

We designed a simple invitation to explore making ink with natural elements. We took advantage of the mild weather and set the invitation in the outdoor studio. We included botanical drawings of flowers as well as flowers we found outdoors. We added a mortar and pestle so the children could grind dry hibiscus flowers before mixing them. Since some of the pigments had to be boiled, we prepared them ahead of time and placed them in mason jars.

We shared the book *Make Ink* to spark children's curiosity and excitement. The experience validated the importance of using books for research to increase children's love for reading and learning. The children had many theories and were thrilled to share them with one another.

The children started by hypothesizing which fruits, herbs, or flowers could be used to create ink and which colors they would make. We shared with the children the inks we had created ahead of time and invited them to test the colors on watercolor paper. We brought out the different spices we tested and invited children to pulverize them using the mortar and pestle and mix them with water.

After a few days of experimenting at making inks of different colors, the children realized that making blue was the hardest. Santiago said, "Blueberries are blue, and they paint my fingers."

Ella, who was always curious and loved the outdoors, suggested that we walk around and find things that were blue. The children took baskets and foraged for anything blue.

Parallel Journey

We gathered and discussed the children's theories and ideas and the results of mixing fruits and flowers to make the color blue. Through additional research, we realized that to get blue, we had to boil the flowers and fruits in a solution of water and baking soda to extract the pigments. We tested boiling blueberries with baking soda and got a deeper blue color than before, but it was still not blue enough. Since it was evident that to produce blue we had to use boiling water, we addressed our concerns about the safety of using boiling water in the proximity of children. Although previously we had preboiled the inks when the children were not present, we weighed the hazards of boiling water with the benefits of letting the children see the process. We looked into licensing limitations too. We decided that the adults would handle the boiling water, but we would do it in front of the children. With meticulous planning and a strong focus on safety, we decided to proceed with the experiment

We introduced an electric plate, explaining its use and the importance of safety to the children. To ensure additional adult supervision, we invited family volunteers. The electric plate was set up outdoors on a table, with chairs placed in a semicircle at a safe distance.

With the children eagerly watching, educator Jessie carefully placed two cups of water in a clear cooking pot and added a spoonful of baking soda. The excitement

was palpable as we all waited to see whether the water would turn the desired shade of blue as it got hotter.

Liam said, "The water is going to pop, pop, pop," as he moved his body to demonstrate how water bubbles when it gets hot.

Noah quietly said, "Dragons make fire."

Diego got a watering can he had been using in the garden and reassured us, "I have water to stop fire."

Emma guessed, "I think hot water will make blue paint." All the children had theories. We asked a couple of the family members to record the children's hypotheses and track their theories in our notebook for the chronicle wall. We watched the children's reactions as the water started to boil and change to a light blue. Harper and Olivia simultaneously said, "It is not strong blue." Emma, always the scientist, proposed a new idea. "The sun helps the flowers be blue. We can use the sun."

Parallel Journey

As we were seeking new ideas for making blue, Miriam shared with Jessie and the other educators that when she made jewelry using copper, heat created greens and blues as the copper oxidized. We decided to explore the idea and discovered that we could place a copper nail in vinegar and water and place it in the sun to oxidize. During the group gathering with the children, we talked about our experiments to make blue and how boiling did not work well enough. We introduce the idea of testing copper in water and vinegar and leaving it outside in the sun. The children decided to tabulate the changes in their nature journals. They also wanted to put the jacaranda flowers and blueberries in water and vinegar and leave them out in the sun. We observed and made notes on the changes we saw. We took photos every day and dated the photos to keep close track

of any changes in color. We added the photos to the chronicle wall for everyone to see.

In the meantime, the children kept mixing and naming different ink colors. We added gum arabic to preserve the ink so we could add it to the paint shelf in the outdoor studio.

After a week, the copper created a deep blue. The children clapped excitedly and decided to name the ink "bluest blue."

Ink Making in Medieval Times

Emma's father, Mathias, a history professor, came into the class to share the history of ink making. He explained how in medieval times, ink was created with oak galls.

The children were familiar with oak galls because we used them in unscripted (Loose Parts) play. They hoped we could find some outside, but we realized that no oak trees lived close to the school, so we would not be able to bring the children to forage for themselves. However, Miriam told us that there were many oak trees in her neighborhood, and she would go foraging for oak galls and send them to the children. A week later, we received a box filled with oak galls that Miriam collected during her daily walks.

Parallel Journey

We read that oak galls are the product of larvae being injected into the tree's branches by a particular species of wasp. The gall provides safety, protection from predators, and nutrients to the wasp larvae. Once the larvae are ready, they drill tiny holes in the gall and free themselves from their temporary home.

We weighed the idea of sustainability and the responsibility of preserving the oak galls so that the wasps could thrive. We decided to present the information to the children to see how they would respond.

We opened the box with the oak galls during a group gathering. We shared with the children what we learned about how the oak galls are created by wasps. They immediately made a connection to the importance of preserving the environment. Aaliyah asked, "Do the oak galls have little holes?" She recognized that the hole meant the larvae had hatched and transformed into a wasp.

Educator Jessie asked, "Why is it important for the galls to have a hole?" Rebecca, the naturalist, immediately responded, "Because the wasp is gone and does not need the oak gall." We proceeded to check every oak gall and found holes in all of them. The children agreed that it was OK to use the oak galls to make ink.

Emma's father, Mathias, returned to help us pulverize the oak galls and boil them to create the ink. He set up a provocation to re-create how people at that time wrote. Jamal, who is constantly curious about how things work and their stories, spent a lot of time each day exploring the feather writers (calligraphy pens simulating feather quills) and the oak gall ink.

In relationship with the natural ecosystem surrounding our campus, the children redefined what art materials and tools could be by utilizing nature and the gifts it offered. Flowers were not simply a beautiful plant or landscape. They were instead material for reimagining designs and bringing natural beauty indoors. Ink was no longer something only found in a marker or pen. It could be created through nature. In seeing themselves as artists, the children discovered new possibilities and methods to express their creative thoughts by using the nature around them.

The children continued to amaze us. Their capacity to understand and make connections showed their capacity to create their own learning. This work was rewarding and engaging. We were learning so much, and we came to work excited and ready to embrace new journeys with the children. We couldn't wait to see what new journeys the children would take us on.

Reflective Questions

- How can you incorporate scientific thinking to guide children's revisiting journeys?
- What strategies can you use to introduce the scientific method to children?
- What assumptions did educators and children make during the ink-making experiments described in this chapter?
- How will you collect data throughout the process of ink making?
- How can you apply critical-thinking skills to evaluate information from the various research sources you've gathered (books, articles, magazines, and videos?

You can also use these questions to deepen children's scientific thinking.

CHAPTER 8

Learning Through Replication

A Journey into Spinners (Spirals) and Mandalas

In this chapter, we highlight how we used chronicle walls to follow the story of children's interest in spinners (spirals) and eventually mandalas (circular designs). The mandalas in this story were more than visual images. They were moments in time; children created them and then deconstructed them to re-create them. In a way, the children's interest in mandalas was a perfect example of a revisiting journey.

This story has many pivoting points, and the educators had to keep track of every idea and every theory that emerged from the children. The educators also engaged in a parallel journey of reflection that helped them honor their commitment to follow the children's interest and to step back, observe, and listen before introducing a concept that would shift the children's revisiting journey.

Replicating Circles

As the children went about their day exploring the natural surroundings of the program, we noticed they were creating circular shapes and spirals using various materials from nature. These replications were happening both outdoors and indoors. To understand their interest, we started photographing their work and capturing their dialogue.

As the children continued playing, we noticed them collaborating on intricate designs. The children interacted and worked together with thoughtful commitment. A sense of altruism and interpersonal relationship was developing. The children became in tune with one another's movements and listened thoughtfully to ideas and propositions. They gave one another permission to trust the creative process. At first their designs were simple. Eventually the children added, changed, and modified their designs to make them more complex. They seemed to be exploring symmetry and patterning. We saw the emergence of mosaiclike structures that were aesthetically beautiful and elegant.

We stepped back and asked ourselves: Was this a natural emergence of mandala designs, and if so, what inspired the children? After reflecting together, we knew that we needed to observe the children's intent further. Were they replicating the physical characteristics of the mandalas, or were they noticing and making connections to circular shapes and patterns? We did not want to step in too fast and take over by setting an invitation that would distract children from their emerging interests.

Parallel Journey

We started by researching the meaning of mandalas and how they emerge in children's play. We wanted to educate ourselves to be ready to guide the children on their revisiting journey.

We studied the work of Rhoda Kellogg, a psychologist who collected and scientifically analyzed approximately one million children's drawings and scribbles. She found that the mandalas emerge everywhere in children's scribbles, and that children draw mandalas entirely on their own, without coaching of any kind. In her classification, she determined that children thirty-six to forty-eight months of age draw mandalas, and that children proceed from mandalas to suns to humans (Kellogg 1969).

Another interest we had was the concept of ephemerality. Children often complete an idea and then destroy it to start again. We wondered whether children were realizing that only some things they valued had to be material, and only some things they created had to be taken home or displayed in the classroom. The process of making art was fulfilling enough to be their focus.

Creating ephemeral art helps children understand the impermanence of ever-changing life. These concepts come naturally to children who spend many hours outdoors. They understand that the seasons, weather, and wildlife are ever-changing.

After discussions, we decided to collect photos of mandalas found in nature and share them with the children. We also looked for books on mandalas that we could share. In the process, we discovered artist Kathy Klein's danmalas (mandalas made from natural materials like cones, leaves, and petals) and were inspired to use natural materials to capture fleeting moments through ephemeral art.

Before introducing new materials to children, we wanted to explore the different materials' affordances. We educators spent an afternoon creating mandalas using natural materials, coloring pencils, and textured papers. This activity was relaxing and mindful and engaged our childhood genius. We let go of expectations and allowed the creative process to guide us, getting us into the flow, that optimal state of performance when work simply flows out without much effort (Csikszentmihalyi 1997). We observed the same flow when the children created their natural replications.

From our play session, we also learned about the power of letting go of expectations. We did not worry about our final products, so we were able to fully relax. We realized that deconstruction is just as important as creation. Through our interaction with transient materials, we discovered the beauty in impermanence and fostered a sense of mindfulness in our creative process. We hushed our internal critics, focusing solely on the present. We realized that our work was not subject to judgment and that we had the liberty to alter it at will. This philosophical exploration of impermanence was a captivating journey, one that truly liberated our creative spirits.

Since the observational data we had collected seemed to lead to multiple possible revisiting journeys, we decided to focus on creating and using the chronicles to keep track of the stories that emerged.

A Family's Invitation to Celebrate Diwali

During the Hindu holiday Diwali, we invited Aurelio's family to share their tradition of making rangoli. Rangoli is an art form that features images and motifs created with colorful powders. The primary purpose of making rangoli during Diwali is to welcome Lakshmi, the goddess of wealth, to individual homes.

Aurelio's family shared with us the meaning of Diwali in their home. We learned that Diwali highlights the love between siblings. They shared with us that on the last day of Diwali, siblings promise to take care of one another and paint a red dot on one another's foreheads. The family also brought colorful sand, shakers, and stencils for us to make rangoli.

As Aurelio shook colored sand onto paper, he shared, "We make these at home. My mama says you have to shake, shake, shake it like this."

Luna added, "I like the purple. Purple is my favorite color. Did you know that purple is Ms. Skye's favorite color too? She told me."

"I wanna make a flower," Ella shared. "It looks like there's flowers on this," she added as she pointed at the stencils in Aurelio's hand.

Malacki noted, "You have to be careful, or when you shake it, it'll go away."

Aurelio responded, "We make it in our backyard. You can do it in your backyard too." Then, gesturing to the outdoor playscape, he added, "This is your backyard, right? You could do it right over there. It's a good spot. Not too sunny."

We followed Aurelio to the spot that he thought was best to create rangoli. He selected a space on the sidewalk, noting, "It's not too dirty. You will see it here." He then demonstrated for us how to use the sifters with the colored sand.

We added sand to the materials in the art studio for children to explore when they were ready. We also added our photos and the children's theories about rangoli to the chronicle wall.

Introducing Photos of Mandalas

Parallel Journey

Since the children had learned about Diwali and rangoli, we wanted to learn more about mandalas as spiritual symbolism. We found photos of the beautiful sand mandalas created by Buddhist monks, so we decided to create sand mandalas ourselves. We wanted to see how children might manipulate sand to create ephemeral art. Miriam remembered gluing colorful sand to coloring books when she was a child. She recalled that it was not easy, but she still remembered the texture of the sand. We learned that sand is incredibly satisfying and relaxing to play with.

We wanted to introduce to the children what we'd learned from our research and play sessions. We created an invitation with photos of mandalas and patterns from nature, as well as the books we'd found during our research. To invite children to replicate this work, we also incorporated sketch paper and coloring pencils. We were curious to see what the children would do and what connections they would make between their designs and the images of mandalas.

Going deeper into our understanding of the connections among mandalas, spirituality, and culture helped us question how to introduce mandalas in ways that honor the cultures who use them in spiritual practices. We didn't want to appropriate a culture or trivialize the meaning of any spiritual practices. For example, when we started creating sand mandalas, learning about the chak-pur tools (conical metal funnels) used by the Buddhist monks was a journey of understanding and respect for us, and we wanted the children to take an equally important journey. We talked to our friends who followed Buddhism to ensure we represented the concepts respectfully and authentically. More importantly, we wanted to instill in the children a respect for mandalas and an appreciation for different spiritual beliefs. Understanding and respecting spiritual beliefs can foster a more tolerant and inclusive society. Though we did not use chak-pur to create mandalas, we asked the children to find a special spot to place the tool.

Throughout the process, we kept stepping back to observe where the children's interests would lead us. We did not want our enthusiasm to guide their thinking, so we continued to hold back introducing the concept of mandala explicitly.

Ella was the first to notice the photographs of the mandalas. She enjoyed exploring and had a deep love of nature and an appreciation for the natural world. The photos captivated her, and she carefully looked at them one at a time. She quietly described the details she saw. We heard her say, "This is round and has lines but is not round and round," as she traced her finger over a photo of the underside of an umbrella. Ella continued to look at the pictures and narrate what she saw: "This flower has many round things."

After a while, Noah joined Ella at the table and started to sort and classify the photos. He separated them first by color and then by similar shapes. He quietly continued the sorting process and listened attentively to Ella's narration. Their quiet back-and-forth symbiosis evolved as they continued their explorations.

A short time later, Luna approached the table and drew a circle on blank paper she'd gotten from the art studio. She looked closely at the photos of spiderwebs and replicated the designs in her drawing. Educator Jessie noticed her drawing and brought colored pencils for her to use. Luna then began to fill each section in a different color. She worked on her design for a long time, but eventually we saw her hesitate about what to do next. Jessie asked, "Luna, do you want to save your drawing to revisit it later?" Luna nodded and handed the drawing to Jessie, who placed it in a basket on a shelf. She reminded Luna that the drawings for revisiting are placed in the basket until the children are ready to continue their work. Then Luna ran outdoors and started to create ephemeral art using natural materials. She collected stones, leaves, and flower petals. She placed the rocks in a circle and carefully filled the center with a complex design using leaves and petals.

Parallel Journey

After our research into Buddhist-inspired symbolic art, we discussed whether we needed to add a new invitation or allow the children to continue to explore the photographs. We asked ourselves, "When should we introduce an invitation to guide the children in noticing the mandalas? Should we ask a question? Should we introduce the concept during group gatherings?" We carefully weighed the pros and cons of moving too fast in the revisiting journey.

Pros	Cons
We can introduce new knowledge to the children.	This new knowledge could limit the children's interest and exert control over their learning.
Some children are ready to make connections and move forward in replicating mandalas. Other children need more time to continue to explore their ideas.	Introducing mandalas could interfere with the natural process of collaboration.

At the end of our discussion, we decided to give the children more time with the photographs and books. We continued to observe to see what connections to the mandalas the children would make. Actively listening to the children's conversations helped us to determine whether we needed to be more intentional in our pedagogy by showing them how their drawings clearly denoted mandalas. We discussed whether we had to let go of our theory that the children were making mandalas and instead spend more time observing and listening to children's conversations and analyzing their drawing further. We knew that we had to make room for the children to guide us. We asked ourselves, "What evidence do we need to validate our theory that the children are exploring mandalas?" We invited one another to ponder this question and conduct more research to share at our next meeting.

The Spiderwebs Appear

A couple of days later, Luna asked Jessie for her drawing. Luna walked to the table with the photographs and found the spiderweb photos. She took them to the platform on the floor and placed them beside her drawing. Luna returned to the table and got a piece of paper and a charcoal pencil. She drew a circle and divided it out with lines. She looked at her original drawing and added a similar design to the new circle drawing. She went to the art studio and got the glue and yarn. We observed her tracing the drawing with glue. She then started cutting pieces of yarn and adding them to the circle drawing until she had covered every line. She looked at her original drawing and spiderweb photos throughout the process. She smiled as she said, "I made a spiderweb."

Parallel Journey

Luna entered the inquiry process through replication. She began by creating a simple flat drawing. She then added complexity, attaching collage materials to incorporate texture. We were curious whether Luna would take the next step and create a fully three-dimensional replication. We also considered possible materials we could introduce into the ecosystem; for example, adding wire might engage Luna in creating different spiderwebs.

We recognized we were at a pivoting point: Some children were redefining their replication and starting to revisit their ideas in different ways. We reviewed our observations and notes. We discussed them during our weekly reflective sessions, and we discovered from the data that we would have to manage the various revisiting journeys the children followed. We agreed to create chronicle journals to capture the individual stories children shared. We also created a new chronicle wall to keep track of the general interests that seemed related to the journeys taking place. The individual chronicle journals were available for both the adults and the children to revisit and add evidence. We invited the children to add their drawings, artifacts, photos, and comments to keep track of their evolving revisiting journeys. The children decided what information they wanted to add to the collective chronicle wall.

During this session, we also played with new materials to go along with Luna's drawings of spiderwebs, including wire, yarn, and thread. We decided that introducing wire would give children a new three-dimensional perspective of spiderwebs. Whenever we introduce new tools to the children, we spend time demonstrating how to use the tool safely. Since this was the first time the children would use wire cutters

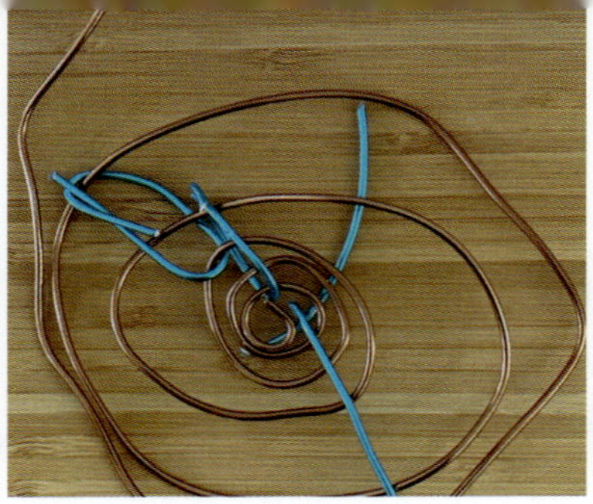

and wire tweezers, we demonstrated their use and then helped the children practice using the tools effectively. We believe that children are capable of learning how to use tools without hurting themselves.

We decided to leave wire and wire tools in the art studio. During a group gathering, we invited Luna to share how she replicated the spiderweb using yarn. The children carefully listened to her story and asked questions. Jessie asked, "What other materials can we use to make spiderwebs?" The children had many suggestions.

Diego: "We can use the big hoops and string."

Aurelio: "We can make them with clay."

Malacki: "We found a big scary spider in my house."

Kamal: "We can make spider costumes."

During the next group gathering, Jessie showed how to use the wire cutters as well as wire tweezers for bending and twisting the wire. Luna, Emma, and Harper began to make spirals by twisting the wire as they created a story about spiderwebs. They drew spiderwebs and scribbled the story underneath the drawing. The wire structures emerged into complex three-dimensional structures. After a while, the three girls added their drawings, stories, and structures to the chronicle wall and the chronicle journal.

"Spinners" Emerge

The children continued to create their intricate designs outside. Many took the photos we provided and brought them outside to replicate. We heard them continuously comment on how they were making circles. Kai, who is incredibly aware of his surroundings, noticed that the children were also making what he called "spinners." We thought he meant spirals. This new term led to a conversation about the difference between circles and spinners. Kai explained that spinners go inside circles. They fill the circle. After sorting the photos for a long time, Noah picked a photo of the fern and the nautilus shell and showed them to the others. Kai exclaimed, "See, a circle with spinners," confirming our guess that Kai's word *spinners* meant "spirals."

Once again, the children surprised us. We admired how they created vocabulary to explain their theories. These comments led to another complex conversation. Ari, the master negotiator and explorer of how things work, excitedly proposed, "Let's hunt for spinners." The children scattered around the yard, and we heard them yell, "I found one!" as they discovered a plant or rock formation that simulated a spinner. Maya suggested taking photos of spinners so they could revisit them later.

Parallel Journey

Maya's suggestion invited us to support the children's hunt for spinners. We decided to get the cameras out so the children could photograph the spinners they discovered. We often use Polaroid cameras because children can view their photos immediately. We were curious about what they would capture and how they would connect the spinners they photographed to the ephemeral art they had been creating.

The next day, during a group gathering, we talked about using cameras. The children had many ideas about what they would photograph next. We wanted the children to collaborate in their hunt for spinners. We asked them to pair up and work together to capture different images of spinners. In our parallel journey of research, we had collected books, photographs, and nature postcards. We brought them out and invited the children to identify spirals. The children spent most of the day taking photos of spinners and sharing them with one another. A natural-born leader, Olivia gathered a small group of children to look at the mandala books. They turned each page until they found what they considered a spinner and took a photo of it. Kai found other spinners to compare the photos to. At one point, Elias noticed that the color wheel was also a spinner. He walked over to the table with various color wheels, and Olivia, Jade, and Maya joined him. They traced their fingers on the color wheel circles and commented on the different colors. They took the color wheel into the art studio, drew circles on white paper, and colored the insides, attempting to replicate the colors in the color wheel.

Once again, we marveled at the children's ability to make connections. They continued to redesign, reflect, and rethink their ideas using the different paint media in the studio.

Parallel Journey

We continued to ponder our mandala theory. Would the children make a connection to mandalas? We observed how children interacted with photos and how the photos influenced the children's designs. Would the children add complexity? Would they combine different materials?

As much as we wanted to present the concept of mandalas to the children, we kept reminding one another of the importance of time and allowing children to explore at their own pace. We wanted them to be in control of their research and learning. We offered multiple opportunities for them to revisit their ideas by using different art media. Luna's interest in spiderwebs reminded us that children can find their creative flow when they have the time and materials to revisit, rethink, and reflect on their theories.

We noticed that the children continued to replicate the spinners using natural materials. They also took photographs of the different creations. Diego, who entered learning through physicality, created large spirals using river rocks in the sandbox.

Starting the Chronicle Wall and Journals

We wanted to ensure children could revisit their photos and grow their thinking about spinners, so we set up a clothesline where the children could hang their drawings, photographs, and theories. (Theories were usually a combination of drawings and letters the children made on a piece of paper to share their ideas.) We added a basket of clothespins children could use to hang their photos.

When we turned control over to the children, we began to notice things we probably would have missed if we educators had controlled the process. Children know their stories and are skilled at highlighting specific moments and sharing their stories in creative ways. We are now in the habit of asking the children if we can add our observations and notations of conversations. This creates a space for research, rethinking, reflecting, and redesigning.

Each child had a unique way of entering into inquiry, but despite different personalities and approaches, we saw intent and respectful collaboration. The central revisiting journey of replicating circular structures and art continued. Each child brought their strengths into the process. Ella, who loved nature, was often seen in the outdoor studio replicating photographs using natural materials. Jamal carefully observed the photographs and explored how to create round structures using wire. He was incredibly skilled at using tools to cut and bend the wire and create what he called "wire spinners." Kai, who was tuned into people's feelings, was always ready to encourage and provide suggestions to peers to accomplish tasks, test solutions, and solve problems. He welcomed peers by providing them with materials, sometimes explaining his actions. Maya loved books. She often recentered herself by reading a book before transitioning to a different space. She was also the keeper of the chronicles. She suggested using nature journals to document their work and often added to her journal and the chronicle wall. She also "read" others' journals.

Maya noticed the mandala books and commented on how other people made spinners and circles. Maya brought the mandala book to the chronicle wall. She looked at the photos of the children's creations and exclaimed, "Look, they look the same!" pointing to a mandala. She turned to Jessie and asked, "What are these called?" Jessie responded, "They are called mandalas. Do you want to learn about them?" A group of children joined as Jessie read a few pages from the book on mandalas. The book sparked new interest in children to create mandalas.

Nature Mandala: Introducing Art as Spirituality

Parallel Journey

Maya's interest in the mandala book inspired us to find a variety of materials children could use to create ephemeral art. We decided it was time to discuss the origin of mandalas and ephemeral art with the children.

During our weekly educators' meeting, we revisited what we knew about mandalas. We discovered the website My Modern Met (https://mymodernmet.com), which provides inspiration, artist biographies, and photographs. We studied the work of Yorkshire artist James Brunt, who uses nature as a canvas for his complex and intricate ephemeral mandalas, infinite spirals, and unique sculptures.

We also revisited the work of Arizona-based artist Kathy Klein. She uses flowers and other organic materials to create inspiringly beautiful mandalas, which she calls danmalas. The term *danmala* originates from the Sanskrit words *dan* and *mala*, which mean "the giver" and "garland of flowers." Kathy Klein uses flowers to create complex circles of symmetry. We thought the children might make connections between the work of Brunt, Klein, and other artists and the sand mandalas they had explored during the celebration of Diwali.

During a group gathering, we showed the children books and a slideshow with the photos from the My Modern Met website. We set baskets of rocks, sticks, and leaves near the outdoor art studio. We also added large wreath-making circles for children to use as bases to create their mandalas. We set out the book *Land Art: Creating Artworks in and with the Landscape* by James Brunt as inspiration. We were excited to see what would happen. We knew the children had already explored nature mandalas, but we trusted they were ready for more intricate designs.

We introduced Kathy Klein's art to the children. We explained symmetry and the idea of creating danmalas. The children were curious and talked about weaving flowers to create garlands. They also started gifting garlands to one another. They called themselves "givers." Since spring was approaching, many trees and flowers were blooming. The children used baskets to collect flowers to design beautiful danmalas. They asked if we could go on walks to collect more flowers and leaves.

Harper, the storyteller, drew intricate details in her art. She enjoyed using unscripted materials to create stories as well. She excitedly started to design danmalas using flowers she foraged. She told a story as she created each one. Her stories were often about giving and her family.

Rebecca's family brought in bouquets from their home garden. Rebecca shared that her mother loved to plant flowers and that Momo (her other mother) liked to cut the grass and collect the fruits from the trees. The children gathered around to see the flowers. Rebecca told them the name of each flower and sorted the flowers by color. Once the flowers were sorted, the children started designing new danmalas. Elias, who loved to mix and create paint, went to the outdoor art studio and started mixing paint to match the colors of the flowers. However, he had no desire to use the paint and instead offered to mix paints for his peers.

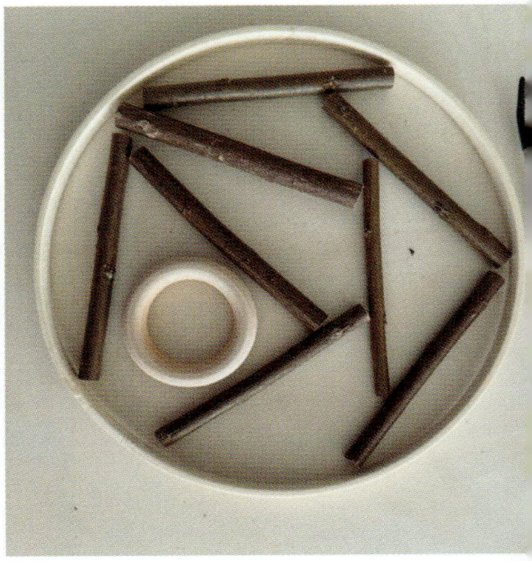

Celebrating Our Learning

We noticed that the children's interest was shifting as their play changed. Some children continued creating mandala-like designs, while others were becoming more engaged with outdoor activities replicating sports. Before the interest in mandalas ended, we wanted to ensure closure and celebration of the children's hard work.

During a group gathering, we asked, "How do we celebrate and share what we learned about mandalas?" The children were used to sharing their learning and were excited to showcase the chronicle wall. The conversation that follows highlights their enthusiasm.

Jamal: "Let's show how things work with the spinners."

Diego: "We can have a mandala show outdoors."

Aaliyah: "We can do a play about mandalas and spin together."

Maya: "We can make a book and read it to our parents."

The children agreed on the idea of making a book about mandalas. Maya went to the chronicle wall, and the other children followed her. They began planning and excitedly shared their ideas.

Maya pointed at the photos and exclaimed, "We need the ones we did!"

Aaliyah, the natural leader, started telling them what to do: "We need to get the photos and paper. Diego, you get the glue."

Kai pitched in and thoughtfully suggested that they could use "strong paper for the book cover."

The educators listened and provided the materials the children needed.

The children decided to have a mandala show and invite the families to create mandalas together. We set to work finalizing the mandala books and the chronicle wall for everyone to see the children's learning. After reflecting and rethinking, the educators reorganized the chronicle journals and created different chronicles for each of the explorations. We then hung the content of the chronicle journals on the walls around the room. Redesigning the chronicle wall allowed us to bring clarity to the learning. It also helped families see how we learned together in the process of the revisiting journey.

The most rewarding part of this journey was the connection children made to ephemerality, realizing that they don't always have to create a lasting product. We know that this will make them more thoughtful and caring consumers.

Reflective Questions

- How do you currently chronicle children's revisiting journeys?
- What types of chronicles (visual journals, chronicle walls) can you create to best tell the story of the revisiting journeys?
- How will you introduce the chronicle process to the children so they become essential to telling the story?
- How do you use the chronicle process to keep track of and make visible children's and adults' learning?

CHAPTER 9

Learning Through Analysis and Evaluation

A Journey into the Local Ecosystem

This chapter focuses on building relationships within the community and exploring the local ecosystem in the natural environment surrounding Jessie's school campus. This journey into nature was designed to spark the children's curiosity about the wildlife, insects, bugs, and animals they encountered. Each of these living beings was unique, with distinct characteristics, making them exciting subjects for exploration and for understanding sustainability. Educators engaged in a parallel journey to strengthen connections with the local community, emphasizing the importance of these relationships in fostering a sense of stewardship for the land. As children deepened their knowledge about sustainability, they learned to value their environment. By observing, assessing, evaluating, and documenting each living creature, we highlighted its unique traits, which enhanced our understanding of

what makes every creature special. Conversations about our local ecosystem inspired a passion for nature and a sense of ethical responsibility to care for the surrounding community.

Exploring the Local Ecosystem

Nature and the outdoors serve an important role in our school community. Rather than viewing our outdoors as a playground, we see it as a learning ecosystem, rich with discovery opportunities and learning experiences for the children. We share with our community of families the importance of nature in our program.

At the start of the school year, we engaged in nature exploration, encouraging the children to explore and discover the outdoor learning ecosystem and all its offerings. We asked the children to take note of what they saw, heard, and smelled, and we invited them to share their discoveries and observations with us at our meeting time.

Rebecca shared, "I wanna show my leaf." Educator Jessie responded, "We would love to know more about your discovery. Why don't you bring your leaf up and share your findings with all of us." Rebecca hopped off the log she was seated on and walked proudly to the middle of the circle with her leaf. She shared, "This is Leafy. I found him over—" She pointed toward a group of trees behind the children. "I brought him to circle 'cuz I wanted everyone to see his little lines. He has little lines on him like my hand." She held up her hand to show her peers. "Do you have a question?" she asked, looking around at her peers.

Diego inquired, "Where was he?"

Rebecca said, "On the ground."

Malacki added, "Where his mommy?"

Rebecca responded, "On the tree. Next question."

Maya said, "I think you should draw him."

Rebecca, turning toward educator Jessie, said, "I need to draw him."

Jessie responded, "That's a wonderful idea. Would you like to leave him here with me and you can draw him when you come back to school tomorrow?"

Rebecca nodded. Maya then exclaimed, "We can all draw him! Jessie, we will need paper and pencils. Oh, and the black thing."

Santiago clarified, "Magnifying glasses."

Parallel Journey

As we listened to the children, we discovered that they had a desire not only to share their discoveries but to document them. They wanted to record their findings to analyze them and then decide what else they wanted to know. The children's request was an invitation for us to consider as we planned the next steps of the revisiting journey. After the discussion, the children went home, and we educators gathered to plan for the following week and discuss how best to honor their request. We also began to wonder what the children were curious about. Why did they want to record this particular leaf? What materials could we provide to support this scientific investigation? How could we support this continued interest? Who in the community could support the children's interest?

We wanted to give children a place to record and revisit and rethink their ideas. We thought about how children might discover the data in their work. We remembered that some of the children returning to the program had started a nature journal the previous year. We decided to reinstate the idea of nature journals for children to record their findings.

We wanted to learn more about scientific inquiry and how scientists develop theories, collect observational data, test hypotheses, and analyze information. We did research to deepen our knowledge of the scientific method and considered how we could share the information with the children. We wanted to encourage children to keep asking questions and to be curious about the local ecosystem.

To learn more about the local flora and fauna in our community, we started our own nature journals and kept a record of our research and findings. We learned so much about the context of the community we live in.

We also planned a nature research lab outdoors. We wanted the children to see themselves as scientists, so we researched what tools and materials are available in a research lab. We asked the families to purchase and donate digital microscopes. We added magnifying glasses, pipettes, eyedroppers, scales and balances, measuring cups and tapes, clipboards, cameras, tongs, brushes, and a basket for the nature journals. We agreed to add more tools as needed.

Designing the Outdoor Nature Research Lab

During the morning gathering, we revisited the children's ideas about recording their scientific findings. We shared with the children how scientists often keep a log, or journal, of their findings. Maya immediately shared, "We can keep our journals near the garden so, so, so when we find something, we can write about it!"

Adding the nature journals in the nature research laboratory sparked further interest in this journey. The children searched the yard for new items to research and record. Inspiration struck again when Santiago suggested expanding their field of inquiry by incorporating the surrounding neighborhood. We discussed with the children what we would need to bring with us. Together we debated whether we should bring our nature journals with us or bring back our specimens and samples for further study in our lab. We decided that we should bring our discoveries back to the school with us so we could view them longer, and, as Harper shared, "to really see all the details."

Parallel Journey

As we listened to the children, we noted they had a desire to analyze and evaluate their findings. They wanted to find the intricate details that lay in each of the nature items they found.

In our reflection meeting, we imagined how we should design our walks to allow the children to revisit their community with a scientific inquiry lens. One way we thought we could deepen this experience was to include the families. Part of our program's vision includes forming meaningful relationships and partnerships with the families. It was our hope that our school could serve as a place of community where we could build lasting connections with families. We thought that working together in scientific inquiry would be an exciting way for families to share their knowledge with the children.

As many of the families lived nearby, we thought about inviting them to join us on an extended neighborhood walk. Recognizing the busy lives that families lead—especially families with young children—we created a survey to find out their availability. We recognized that their schedules would vary and agreed that we should select the date and time that allowed for the most participants to join us. This invitation was not exclusive to the direct parents or guardians but also included extended family members and other important adults in the children's lives. By casting a wider net, we hoped to strengthen our own relationships, facilitate new connections in our community, and support the children's continued inquiry.

Planning the Scientific Research Walks

We shared our scientific adventure date with the children and families. We knew that we still had more planning to do with the children. As scientists, it is important to imagine possibilities and plan accordingly. Jessie asked the children, "How will we transport our specimens back to our nature laboratory?"

Diego suggested, "Let's bring buckets."

Santiago said, "But they might not be big enough. What if we find a whole tree part?"

Emma, looking inquisitively at Santiago, said, "Do you mean a stump?" She then got up from the stump she was sitting on, pointed at it and said, "Like this?"

Santiago said, "How will we get it back here? It won't fit in a bucket."

Austin, raising a finger in the air, excitedly exclaimed, "I know! I know! I know! Let's bring the wagon. We can put stuff in it. The big stuff. And we can still use our buckets too." It was decided. We needed to bring buckets, baskets, and the wagon to transport the discovered materials back to our nature research lab.

On the day of our walk, the children found many specimens they wanted to examine further, including pine cones and seedpods. Bringing the samples back prompted a deeper desire to analyze their intricacies, discover their properties, and determine what made them unique.

Pine Cones and Bugs

When we got back to our lab, the children used the magnifying glasses to examine our findings. After holding the magnifying glass close to a pine cone, Jamal said, "We need to get inside of the pine cone. I wanna see inside it."

Jessie asked, "How do you think we can do that?"

Jamal was quiet for some time, continuing to examine the pine cone from all angles. He held it above his head and spun it around, using the magnifying glass to look at each individual crevice. After the third time doing this, he said, "We can cut it?"

Jessie responded, "How?"

Jamal laid the pine cone on its side, lifted his hand, and began making a sawing motion with the edge of his hand, suggesting, "I think right here."

Jessie then asked, "What do you think we need to use to cut it?"

Jamal exclaimed, "Scissors!"

Austin, who was busy using a magnifying glass to look at his sketches in his nature journal, said, "No. You need a saw. My daddy uses a saw. He makes it go like this." He then waved his hands frantically back and forth in a straight line and added, "Then, he's done."

Jessie asked Austin's dad, Roberto, who had gone on the walk, to help the children dissect the pine cone. Roberto went to his car to retrieve his tools while the children gathered, excited to see what was inside the pine cone.

While examining the guts of the pine cones, Santiago pondered aloud, "Where are the bugs?" The children pivoted, and their interest moved to explore bugs.

Parallel Journey

Santiago created a new line of inquiry for the children. They began to question where the bugs lived. We knew that we wanted to encourage this deeper connection, so we reflected on how we could do this.

In our parallel journey reflective meeting, we discussed Santiago's question, "Where are the bugs?" We reflected on the materials available to the children in the nature research laboratory and decided we needed to reimagine the space to extend the children's line of inquiry. We decided to provide additional tools as opposed to redesigning the whole space. We thought about what tools we could offer the children. We added real binoculars to aid the children in their search for bugs.

We weren't sure where this new line of inquiry would lead. Drawing on our program's philosophy of being collaborators and researchers with the children, we knew that we would need to pay careful attention to the children's actions and conversations to know how best to support this journey the children were on. We also wanted children to think about sustainability and respecting their natural community's ecosystems, including bugs. We wanted them to know that it was essential to examine the bugs carefully to keep them alive.

We introduced binoculars in a morning meeting. While a few of the children were familiar with the tool, it was new to many of them. They shared their theories about how to use binoculars and how to care for them to prevent them from breaking or getting scratched.

Santiago said, "You look in them like this and see things," moving his hands to create circles around his eyes.

Diego shared, "You put them on your eyes."

Ella proclaimed, "You have to wear them like this!" She gestured around her neck. "You have to be careful because they're fragile."

"Fragile!" Noah exclaimed.

"So we don't throw them," Kai reasoned to the group.

Santiago and Diego were the first to pick up a pair of binoculars. Ella accompanied them as they began scouring the outdoor classroom. Ella spotted some *Armadillidium vulgare* (roly-polies) near the entrance gate. "Over here!" she said. Ella squatted down and picked up a roly-poly. She held her arm straight out to Santiago and Diego as the roly-poly crawled up the back of her hand.

"I can't draw him," Santiago said. "He moves too fast."

Diego said, "Bring him back to the lab. Let's put him on the table." Diego and Santiago sprinted back to the lab while Ella carefully walked, balancing the roly-poly on her arm. Once at the laboratory, she plucked the roly-poly off her arm and placed it on the table. It immediately started crawling away.

Diego said, "He's leaving! Stop him." Santiago placed the binoculars down in the roly-poly's path. This only prompted the roly-poly to turn and try to go around them. Ella placed the magnifying glass in its path, but again to no avail. The roly-poly crawled off the edge of the table and landed on its back. Ella picked up the

roly-poly and placed it back on the table. This process continued as the children attempted to "capture the roly-poly," as Diego exclaimed, so they could "study him," according to Ella. It presented an opportunity to discuss how to carefully examine bugs without hurting them. We talked about observing the roly-polies in their natural habitat and not moving them to the lab. We discussed with the children how they could take photos to analyze and draw instead of trying to capture live specimens.

Parallel Journey

Ella brought forth a pathway in the children's journey of analysis and evaluation. We now knew the children's desire to chronicle their surroundings was extending from nature materials to living things. The question we pondered was how to provide the children with an invitation to explore living things in their natural habitat without moving them. Living creatures pose a challenge because they move about, crawl, and fly away. However, the children wanted to evaluate and assess the different features of the roly-polies. We decided to take a risk and provide the children with preserved insects and bugs in specimen cases, rather than moving the bugs they encountered. We again redesigned the nature research laboratory, incorporating the preserved specimens with microscopes. We invited the children to record their findings in their journals. We encouraged them to look at the finer details and characteristics of the specimens to determine which features made them unique. We researched the scientific names of all the specimens to share with the children. We hoped to instill in children respect for living things.

We offered the children preserved specimens of insects living in our community. While we began with small bugs, we quickly expanded to butterflies and ladybugs, which were beginning to appear in our outdoor ecosystem.

The children diligently recorded their findings, noting the insects' different body parts.

Ella proclaimed, "These are its feets. It has lots of little feets." She gestured with her fingers to replicate the legs.

Diego inquired, "Are those its eyes? Where are its eyes?"

Jade asked, "Is it a mommy?"

We knew then that we needed to engage in further teacher research.

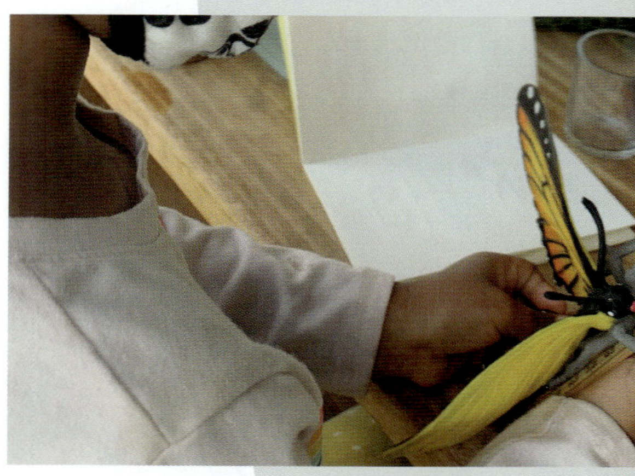

Parallel Journey

We looked for more information about the insects. We researched where they lived, what time of year we were most likely to observe them, how they formed colonies, and what they ate. We included the children in this process. The children chronicled their findings in their nature journals,

expanding upon their initial observations with this new information.

The Snake Encounter

The children's interest in the wildlife surrounding our school continued throughout the year. As we were located near a canyon, a variety of animals graced our campus. The most exciting animal we saw was a nonpoisonous snake. This friendly snake entered our outdoor environment during the children's lunch. The visitation created much conversation and excitement in the children. Knowing this was a spontaneous and fortuitous opportunity, we engaged the children in conversation to see what their interests were regarding this visitor. We asked the children to share their thoughts about the snake.

Ari: "Where's he going?"

Aaliyah: "Maybe he's going home. He just wanted to make friends."

Liam: "Why'd he leave too fast?"

Malacki: "I think he wanted to go back to his family."

Jade: "I think he was the daddy snake, and he has to get back to his baby."

Kai: "Yeah. He wants to be with his baby."

Emma: "Is he a nice snake?"

Jovani: "I actually saw the snake, and it has a flat surface on the top of its head. That means he lives near my house."

Jade: "I saw the eyes, the head, and the mouth. But where he live?"

Parallel Journey

We noticed that the children seemed most curious about where the snake lived and whether it had a family. While we knew the snake most likely lived in the nearby canyon, we also knew that more research was needed to satisfy the children's questions. Simply responding that the snake probably lives in the canyon would not have afforded the children the opportunity to investigate it further. It would have ended the conversation and journey. We decided first to investigate what type of snake had visited us. We wanted to include the children in this process. We decided that the best method to do this would be at our next morning meeting, as the snake's visit occurred at the end of our school day.

The next morning, we came prepared for our meeting with the children. We brought our tablet loaded with images of common snakes of San Diego to support the children in rediscovering their interest in the snake from the previous day. We encouraged the children to reflect and think back to the special visitor. We asked the children, "What did you notice about the snake yesterday? What distinct features did you see?"

Jade shared, "The snake looks kind of thickly. It was kind of scabbling." Jessie asked Jade to clarify. "Thickly" was Jade's way of communicating that the snake's skin was thick. By "scrabbling" she meant that the skin had a lot of marks on it and that it was frayed.

Aaliyah, placing her finger to her chin, stated, "I saw the head. It was really big. It was kind of brown and yellow with squares on it."

Emma said, "It was like scary." She then wrapped her arms around her body and shivered.

Kai, looking at Emma, said, "It's OK. He won't hurt us. He has a baby snake. He was just going back to his baby."

Ari added, "The snake was this long." He spread his arms as wide apart as possible. He shared, "It was

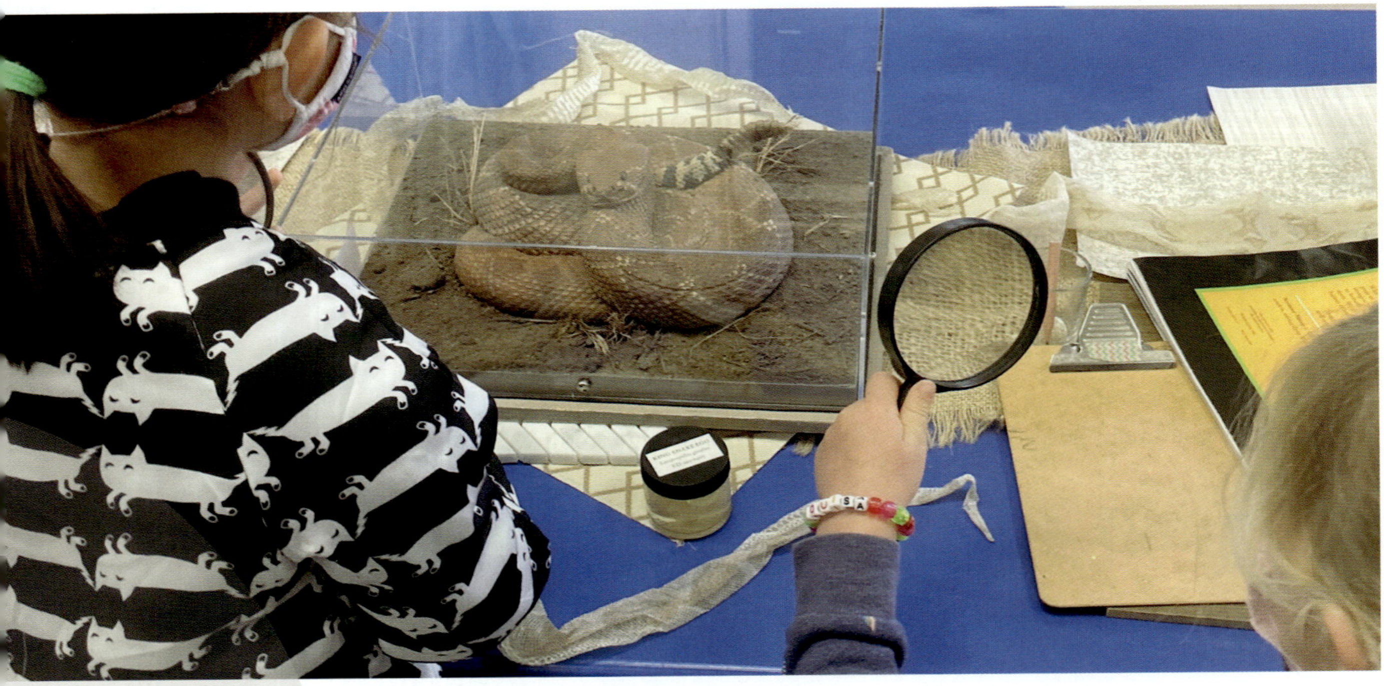

probably like fifty feet. That's why he was the daddy snake, because he was so long. Oh yeah, and one more thing. He was kind of brown. Maybe a little tiny bit yellow."

Malacki asked, "Was it a rattlesnake? I didn't see a rattle. My brother has a rattle. He goes, 'Wah, wah, wah,' and Mama gives him the rattle."

Jessie shared, "It was not a rattlesnake. There was not a rattle on it. But you make a good point. It did look like a rattlesnake."

We began the process of discovering the type of snake that visited us by asking the children, "How should we search for the snake?" While most of the children suggested looking online for the word *snakes*, Jovani said, "Search *San Diego snake*." Various images of snakes came up, including a California kingsnake, a Southern Pacific rattlesnake, a San Diego gopher snake, and a garter snake. After comparing and contrasting the images online to the distinct features of the snake in our yard, we discerned that a San Diego gopher snake, a nonvenomous snake, had been our visitor.

Parallel Journey

We chronicled the children's observations and questions from both of our meetings. We reviewed the data to determine what questions the children had so we could determine the pathway we should take. The children had shared many observations and thoughts about the snake, but the recurring questions continued to center on where the snake lived and whether it had a family.

We educators knew that it was essential to teach the children about snake safety. San Diego is home to a variety of snakes—both venomous and nonvenomous. During our reflective weekly meeting, we researched types of snakes we could encounter on our walks. We wanted to offer children scientific knowledge while telling them to proceed with caution when they encountered a snake.

Since we now knew that a gopher snake had visited us, we decided to research more information about gopher snakes. We found books at the local library and obtained specimens from the San Diego Natural History Museum. We used the books and specimens to redesign the outdoor nature lab.

From our research, we learned that snakes are most active during the day. They can be found in backyards, outdoor classrooms, and around our neighborhood, as they commonly live in the canyons and brush along the coast of San Diego. Our books told us that snakes lay eggs and do not typically stay together as a family.

During a group gathering, Jessie described a real experience she'd had when a snake visited her home. Jessie lived in a canyon, and she was lucky enough to have had a snake visit her backyard a few weeks earlier. She explained that even though she was afraid of snakes, she recognized that her visitor offered an opportunity to extend the children's journey into analysis and evaluation, and she decided to be brave and snap a few pictures of the snake in her backyard. She shared the pictures with the children during a group gathering. The children had many hypotheses about what type of snake it was. They looked at books and decided that the snake that visited Jessie was a racer snake, and it was not venomous.

The children compared and contrasted Jessie's snake with the one that had entered our campus. In this process, they were rediscovering their curiosity about the ecosystem surrounding our campus.

Jovani: "The school snake was kind of brown and kind of yellow."

Ari: "He was really, really long! This snake looks kind of like a little short. I think he's short. Is he short?"

Malacki: "Is this the same snake? Is he your pet, Jessie?"

Aaliyah: "He's not her pet. He's outside and not on a leash. We always put our dog on a leash."

Jovani: "He can't be the same snake. That's too far. Unless, Jessie, do you live here? Like do you live inside school?"

Malacki: "Was it a rattlesnake this time?"

Jessie explained that she did not live inside the school and that the snake in her yard was not a rattlesnake either. She asked the children what else made them believe it was a different snake. The children analyzed the features of the snake from Jessie's backyard in comparison to the snake that had entered their playscape. We invited the children after the reflection meeting to journey further into their analysis of the two snakes, and we started a chronicle wall to keep track of our findings.

We placed the photo of Jessie's snake in the nature lab along with a rattlesnake specimen we'd procured from the San Diego Natural History Museum. We hoped the children would compare, contrast, analyze, and evaluate the similarities and differences among the snakes. We invited the children to chronicle their findings just as they had with the snake that visited the school.

In revisiting their sketches of the snake that visited the school, the children observed that they used a lot of brown and yellow colors. Ari again noted, "This snake [Jessie's snake] is more green in the picture. I need some greens. It's more green and kind of brown and black. There's lots of black. I didn't use black last time." Using a magnifying glass to examine the photo of Jessie's snake and his drawings, he stated, "Yep! This is definitely not the same snake. Look! You can see it here." He pointed at his drawings.

Kai observed, "This one has circles on it." He waved his hands around excitedly in a circle.

Ari added, "I see the tail . . . and the head. The head is really little. It's black and kind of green. The other one was more yellow."

Rebecca noted, "Look at its eyes! They look like black dots."

Jamal asked, "Where are the eyes? I don't see the eyes!"

Noah shared, "There on the side of him. It's his eye. He's looking at us. I look for pictures too. My mama says smile. He's not smiling at us."

Olivia said, "I see the mouth." Then, giggling, she added, "Ahhhh! He's going to eat me!"

Diego noted, "I actually see little spikes going out of the snake. It's like a flat surface on the top and it looks like a volcano."

Ella, with supreme confidence, stated, "It's stripes with dots in them."

By revisiting their previous work, the children were able to refine their knowledge of snakes.

A short while later, Jessie found a snake skin in her backyard. Again, recognizing the opportunity that this presented to the children, she got over her own fear, put on disposable gloves, and placed the snake skin in a sealed

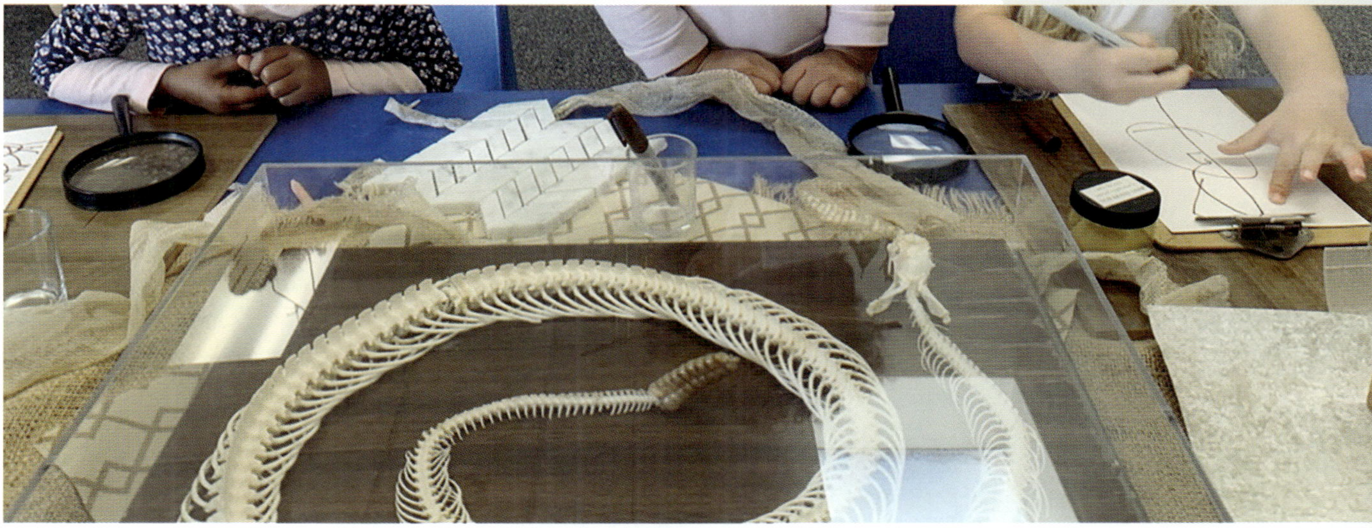

zip-top bag and brought it to school. At school, she transferred it into a specimen container for the children to examine and analyze.

Parallel Journey

We wondered how the children would react to the snake skin. First we kept it in a jar, but soon we thought it was time to let the children touch it and explore it in more depth. The children had determined that the snakes were different by evaluating the snakes' bodies. We were curious to see what questions the children would bring forth about the snake skin and what observations they would make. We again decided to redesign the nature lab by adding the snake skin and putting back the microscopes, which we had used earlier in the school year.

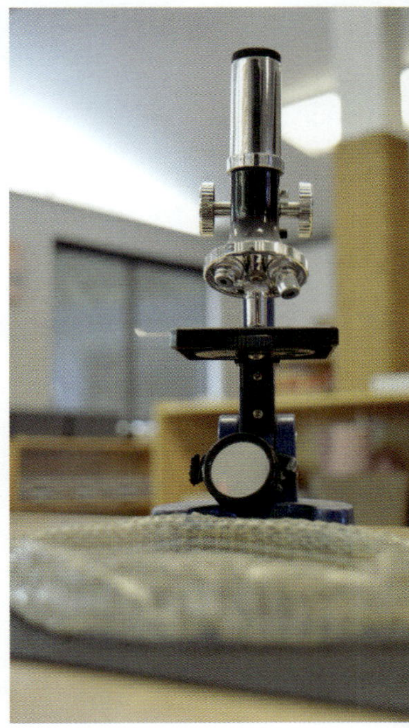

Jamal: "Inside is where the snake used to be. I wanna see it come out! I wanna see it come out of its skin."

Diego: "Don't these snake skins look cool?"

Harper: "Are there water snakes?"

Noah: "Hahahahaha! Toilet snakes."

Ari: "Look! It's kind of moving. It felt like a snake. Why is the tail wiggling?"

Aaliyah: "It feels like . . . scary. I think that snake is dead."

Emma: "It's too scary. I don't want to touch it."

Ari: "It feels squishy."

Jovani: "Is it real? Is it dead? Did it die?"

Santiago: "What's his name?"

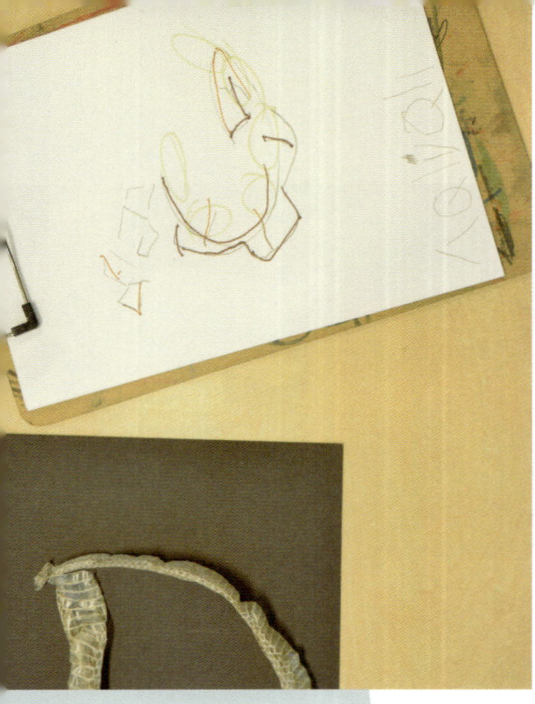

Parallel Journey

The children were focused on whether the snake skin meant the snake had died. So we decided to research snake skin, including why and how it is shed. We returned to the library for more books on snakes. We learned that snakes shed their skin in one continuous piece between four and twelve times a year. The process of shedding their skin is called ecdysis. We researched with the children what this process entails. We discovered that just prior to shedding, the snake's skin begins to turn bluish, and its eyes become opaque, hindering vision. Within a few days, the snake rubs its head on something abrasive, like a rock, to tear open the outer layer of skin. It then works on the tear, crawling through tight quarters, sliding out of the skin, leaving the old skin inside out—much like a child peeling off a sock. The process can take from days to a couple of weeks, depending on size, body condition, and environment.

We encouraged the children to revisit the snake skin and chronicle any new findings they had. Ella noted, "I think I see a blue tail. I'll tell you what—like on the sides, it feels thickly. The snake skin is kind of scrabbling a little. When I look closer, it looks bigger."

The children again chronicled their findings. They engaged in peer review with one another, looking over one another's drafts and providing feedback and suggestions for further attributes and characteristics they could add to capture the details of the snake skin. In this process, the children revisited their abilities to analyze and evaluate data.

While looking at Aaliyah's interpretation, Harper noted, "You needa add the circles. Those are the scales. It needs more scales."

The children continued to create drafts of the snake skin, using a variety of materials to finalize their representations.

Parallel Journey

The children's ability to analyze and evaluate their surroundings showed us the deep relationship they had with nature. This work helped us see the connections the children made with the natural ecosystem surrounding our campus. They observed and thought critically about the living creatures they encountered, deepening their relationship with and understanding of the

importance of preserving and conserving nature. This journey was filled with joy and challenged us as educators to step outside of our own comfort zones to provide invitations for the children to deepen and continue their journey.

Reflective Questions

- What do you know about your local community and its ecosystems?
- How can you explore your local community ecosystem with the children?
- How can you create a shared understanding with the children of what a community ecosystem is?
- What resources are available in your community? How can you engage community resources to help you collect tools that support the revisiting journey?
- What can you do to expand your relationships with essential community stakeholders?

CHAPTER 10

Learning Through Representation

A Journey into Identity Through Stitching Stories

In this chapter, educators Jenny Gallego and Taylor D'Auria from Kinderoo Children's Academy tell their own story of embarking on parallel journeys with children focused on identity development—specifically, nurturing children's identities as creators, artists, and learners. A positive and healthy identity is rooted in the relationships between adults and children. Identity is crucial for social-emotional development and forms the foundation of a child's sense of self and well-being. When children feel they belong and are allowed to explore their interests and ideas, they are more likely to develop a sense of agency and discover their identities as learners and creators.

Founded in 2003, Kinderoo Children's Academy in Ocala, Florida, embraces a Reggio-inspired approach, enriched with blended theories and philosophies from around the world that value children's natural interests and creativity. Part of the practice of the Kinderoo educators is to gather weekly

to review, revisit, and reflect on what happened throughout the preceding week. This community of practice and learning includes the parallel journey of adult play, in which the educators come together to engage in meaningful play experiences, creating a supportive and collaborative environment. This model has been an ongoing process and is built into the culture of the program. Regular meetings, workshops, and play sessions ensure that learning and collaboration continue to evolve within the educators' practice.

At the beginning of each school year, we work to build a compassionate classroom community by strengthening everyone's identity and self-love. In the five-and-six-year-olds classroom, we introduce self-portraits to the children to begin a dialogue about who they are. The children study themselves and their unique characteristics and create representations of themselves by working with unscripted materials that are similar to their features.

Parallel Journey

As educators, we often spend time reflecting on the meaning of identity and how we can support children in developing a healthy sense of who they are as creators, learners, and humans. Self-portraits are significant in children's identity development. Research evidence shows that by age four, children can see themselves as possessing general traits they represent in their art.

We are influenced by Loris Malaguzzi's philosophy, which views self-portraits as reflections of the personality in a visual, physical, and psychological sense. Self-portraits become a mediator of communication with the self, a medium of self-investigation. In this way, the self-portrait exists as a means of self-reflection, self-awareness, and acceptance of the self (Malaguzzi and Musatti 1996). We also read the book *The Language of Art* by Ann Pelo (2017). This validated our belief that self-portraiture is deeply connected to children's identity perception.

During our weekly play meeting, we discussed the role of educators in providing children with the necessary tools and materials to create self-portraits that truly represent their identities. This involves creating a safe space for them to explore and introducing new tools to help them communicate their ideas and perceptions of themselves. With the idea of exploring our own identities, we created our own self-portraits. We mixed spices and paints to match skin tones.

This led to a dialogue about how to initiate meaningful conversations about identity with the children that would encourage reflection and curiosity. We wrote inquiry questions aimed at stimulating meaningful dialogue, encouraging self-discovery, and empowering children to express themselves authentically through their self-portraits:

1. "What are some special or unique things about yourself? What makes you you?" We wondered if these questions would encourage children to reflect on their individual qualities, talents, and interests.

2. "How do you feel when you look in the mirror?" We wanted children to explore their emotions, look deeper into their self-perception (how they see themselves and how others may see them differently), and understand the connection between inner feelings and outward appearance.

3. "What do you like most about yourself?" We were curious if this question would prompt children to identify their strengths, promoting self-confidence and self-love.

Next, we curated a collection of books to support self-portrait making. We envisioned an interactive environment, buzzing with dialogue and inquiry as the children interacted with new materials. We discussed reading the children a book during the group gathering and researched artists' works on self-portraiture, taking inspiration from Vincent Van Gogh's self-portrait.

Exploring Identity with Colors and Mirrors

We introduced the children to a skin color exploration involving mixing spices and paints, and comparing the colors to their skin. The children were quick to notice the diversity of skin colors among them and to understand how they needed to mix spices and paints to match their skin colors. We preserved the mixtures they created so they could use them for their self-portraits. These explorations would help the children to understand that their skin color is a part of their identity and should be honored and celebrated.

Parallel Journey

We educators gathered for our weekly play meeting. This time, we played with mirrors and looked at ourselves from different angles. We wanted to explore how our perceptions of self changed depending on the angle. Since we often explore the properties of light and use technology and digital media to enhance children's play and learning experiences, we now explored ways to trace our bodies onto paper. We wanted to incorporate projections and digital tablets to visually engage children with the concept of symmetry found in art and nature.

We placed mirrors throughout the classroom, offering a variety of angles for self-reflection, and we offered magnifying glasses to provide opportunities for close examination. We also created digital projections of the children's photographs and made available a digital tablet for drawing, researching, and chronicling the revisiting journey. The intention for these learning contexts was to prepare the children to engage creatively and promote philosophical discussions about diversity and inclusion. This interactive learning environment was designed to keep them excited, engaged, and actively involved in their own learning process.

To introduce the mirrors, we read the book *In the Mirror* by Fabian E. Ferguson, which promotes resilience, positivity, and appreciation for who you are. This book prompted the children to look in the mirrors and explore their reflections. This helped us discover how the children perceived themselves. We asked them, "When you look in the mirror, what do you see?"

We noticed a group of children drawing only one half of their bodies. We wondered why the children were exploring only one side of their bodies. Were they attempting to understand symmetry? Would they connect both sides of their bodies?

Parallel Journey

Not having experience with symmetrical art, we decided to reflect on it and reframe our next steps to provoke further inquiry. In our next meeting, we spent time exploring symmetry and discussing how the symmetry we find in our own bodies is connected to the concepts of proportions, patterns, shapes, balance, art, and beauty.

We researched artists who incorporate symmetry into their art. We studied the art of Leonardo da Vinci, who explored symmetry in the human body. One famous example is *The Vitruvian Man*, a drawing that illustrates the proportions of the human body within a square and a circle.

We talked about how to introduce the concept of symmetry to the children in connection with their own identities. We looked at works of art that showed symmetry. We wondered how we might utilize technology and other tools, such as a video projector, to enhance their understanding of symmetry and mathematical concepts while creating self-portraits.

To prepare for this new encounter, we printed photographs of the children and cut them in half. We wondered how children would explore the concept of symmetry in their own images. Would the children's self-portraits evolve once they recognized the symmetry in their own features and bodies? Would this help them better understand who they are?

Exploring Symmetry in Our Features and Bodies

During a group gathering, we introduced the photographs we had cut in half. We invited children to draw mirror images to create the missing halves. This exploration encouraged the children to deeply explore the facets of their physical appearance that made up their identity while practicing artistic skills. We celebrated our own beauty and the nuanced details that make us unique. Additionally, the children practiced essential math skills such as using a ruler, understanding bilateral symmetry, recognizing patterns, and identifying whole, half, equal parts, and the middle line. Witnessing the children's growth and development engaged our curiosity and led us to think of the next steps in this revisiting journey of identity.

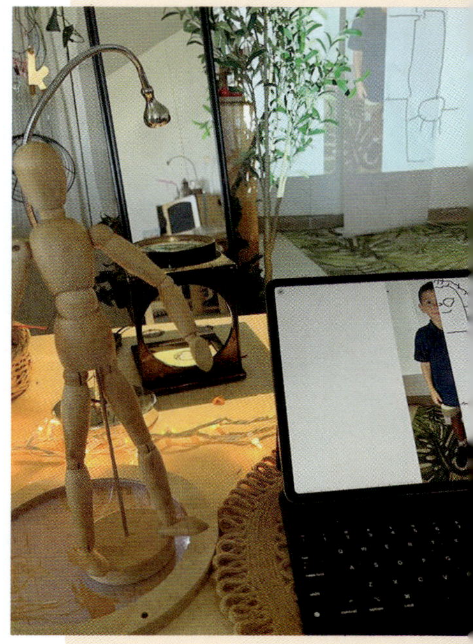

As the children explored with mirrors and their photographs, their comments and discoveries painted a picture of their identity. As Krysten observed a projection of half of her own photo, she said, "I'm missing one part of me." She went to the whiteboard where half of her photo was projected and began to complete the other half. She drew a leg, measured it with a ruler, and noticed how her leg was not at the same level as the other one. Using her critical-thinking skills, she erased it and drew it again, making sure they were the same length (symmetrical). She made an imprint of the left hand and compared how the right and left hand have symmetry. Afterward, she observed the portraits other children were creating, noticing the differences with her own. In comparing and contrasting her own portrait with those of her peers, Krysten was able to fine-tune her ideas about her identity and what makes her uniquely her.

The educators projected the photographs as children requested them. Luis immediately became curious and exclaimed, "In the mirror, I can see my face, my belly, and my legs' movements! In my shadow, I see all my body—I don't in the picture." He began to play with his shadow, comparing it with the projected picture. Anita looked at herself in the mirror and said, "I love my picture. My body has a line in the middle." She drew the other half of her body, "Now I can see my face, my arm, and my leg . . . also my shoe."

The conversations were lively, and we recorded them individually for revisiting later. Damian also connected the concepts of symmetry and identity when he noticed that part of him was missing and began to draw the other half. Eduardo's active engagement was also evident, as he used his mathematical thinking and understanding of symmetry to recognize, "This is the hand that is missing." He then went to the digital tablet and, using a ruler, began to measure his body. He drew the other half of himself, paying attention to the line where his body was divided (between legs, neck, and head). He came back to the projection and, using his shadow, verified his body; his identity was now complete. After observing herself in the mirror, Maritza drew herself using different colors to make her other half. She then painted a heart next to her portrait, exclaiming, "I love myself!"

As the children revisited identity concepts, we noticed a continued interest in examining their faces and bodies closer in the mirror. In revisiting their reflections, the children began to take note of their own expressions. They connected their facial expressions to their emotions, such as happy, sad, silly, and angry, seeing that emotions were a part of their identities.

Parallel Journey

In our weekly community of practice, we shared our notes and observations. We noticed that starting with self-portraits allowed children to understand that their identity goes beyond physical appearance. It includes abstract concepts such as the inner self, emotions, and expressions.

We wanted to encourage the children's exploration of self-identity, as this can help children learn more about one another and foster a sense of community. We made a point of addressing children's emotions as they emerged in conversation. We'd observed the children's fascination with examining their faces and bodies in the mirror, exploring how various facial expressions link to emotions, which is a crucial step in developing emotional literacy. This observation prompted us to delve deeper into several inquiries within the revisiting journey:

- How are emotions connected to our own identity?
- How can we further enrich the children's emotional literacy (their ability to read and respond to their emotions and other people's emotions) through self-portraits?

We were keen to expand discussions around diversity and inclusion by examining various aspects of identity and representation in self-portraits. We aimed to involve families in this process not only to strengthen the connection between home and school, but also to help children see how their home life is another aspect of their identity. We also considered strategies to engage children who initially struggled with self-expression or observation in the self-portrait process. Furthermore, we contemplated introducing alternative creative mediums or techniques to allow children to express their identities beyond traditional self-portraits. Finally, we were interested in assessing the impact of the self-portraiture project on children's self-perception, confidence, and overall well-being.

Through careful observation and dialogue, we could see that this exploration of self-reflection in the mirror provided a valuable opportunity for the children not only to develop emotional literacy but also to enhance their self-awareness and self-esteem. By recognizing and interpreting their facial expressions, they were actively engaging in the process of understanding and regulating their emotions, a crucial skill for social and emotional development. Moreover, our parallel journey of self-discovery opened doors for discussions on topics like self-identity, body positivity, and acceptance, fostering a supportive and inclusive classroom environment.

As educators, we seized this opportunity to encourage discussions around diversity and individual uniqueness, reinforcing the idea that every child's journey of self-discovery, of identity, is valid and worthy of celebration. Through reflection and inquiry, we continued to explore ways to nurture and support each child's journey of self-discovery, recognizing the profound impact it has on their overall well-being and holistic development.

Introducing Fabric to Create Self-Portraits

As the children continued exploring, we invited them to create their final self-portrait in our series. The children took their time using markers to draw their faces onto fabric. We encouraged them to use a mirror and photographs of themselves as a guide. As they drew, each child paid special attention to the shape of their face, eyes, mouth, and nose. Once they were finished, we encouraged them to describe themselves. Finally, we invited the children to embroider their portraits with yarn, choosing the colors that best matched with their features. They created their self-portraits with precision, paying attention to the smallest details that they hadn't noticed at the beginning of the project, such as their eyelashes, ears, and skin color. Throughout the process, the children expressed how they felt and thought about themselves.

Emiliana: "I love my hair. I feel happy about myself." She worked with different colors and used the mirror to compare the colors of the thread with her hair and features. She then chose the most accurate colors.

Angelica: "My eyes are little, also my nose and my boca [mouth]. My hair is blonde and bright." Angelica began to use some Spanish words from our Spanish lessons as she described herself.

Anita: "I feel happy and loved."

Parallel Journey

We reviewed our notes, and we thought that since the children had been exploring fabric to make self-portraits, we could introduce new tactile media to them. We recognized the valuable role that tactile media play in developing fine-motor skills and hand-eye coordination. We decided to start teaching children the art of sewing. First, we wanted to ask what the children knew about how cloth is made.

In our morning dialogue session, we asked the children about the origins of cloth and how it is made. We talked about how what we wear is part of our identity. We started by asking, "Did you know that materials have an identity? They have an origin and beginning like you. Where do yarn, string, and sewing threads come from?"

Greyson: "From Ms. Martha [our director]."
Angela: "From a pillow."
Emiliano: "From recycled materials."
Selena: "Feels like a blanket."
Kattleia: "From animals."
Joziah: "From grass."
Amelia: "Sheep's wool."
Kinsley and Julian: "From trees and wood."
Levi: "From fluff balls."

Parallel Journey

To prepare for an in-depth exploration of sewing materials, we checked out books from our school library and solicited ideas from our colleagues and families to ensure we would instill inquiry, wonder, and curiosity. We wrote a plan to help us project possible experiences and learning contexts:

- Material gathering: We thought about how to help children make the connection between the origins of the materials and their own origins. We gathered a diverse range of resources, including natural fibers, yarn, and thread. We shared basic stories of where materials such as cotton and wool originate. We asked families to share stories with their children as well, to make the connection between home and school.

- Skill-building workshops: We engaged in a tools-and-materials workshop with other colleagues at the school to better understand the affordances and use of these items. We also consulted with families who could give us demonstrations of their skills.
- Environment setup: We designed the classroom environment to facilitate both dialogue and experiences. We set up books and photographs for inspiration along with the tools and materials necessary for sewing and weaving, ensuring each child had access to an individual workspace. This setup was designed to encourage participation and allow autonomy.
- Safety guidelines: Recognizing the importance of safety when children are working with needles and other sewing tools, we prepared a set of safety guidelines. We began sessions by demonstrating how to handle sewing equipment.

By taking these preparatory steps, we aimed to create a rich educational environment where children would gain insight into their own origins through the art of sewing.

After having an interactive discussion about the origins of yarn and thread, we read books and shared educational videos. To deepen the children's understanding, we explored the full life cycles of these materials, from the natural sources, like cotton plants and sheep's wool, to the processes that transform these raw fibers into usable threads.

We presented the children with several learning contexts to explore the new art medium with their senses. We discussed how our senses are a part of us and our identity. We explained that we need to use our senses to better understand the identity of these materials.

We asked, "What does the new material feel like in your hands? How can you manipulate it with different types of weaving tools? What sound does it make when you use it on different surfaces? What do you feel when you use the material with a stick, or a needle, or your hands?"

To answer our evolving questions, the children began a hands-on investigation.

Kaylyn touched the textures of several types of yarn and threads, noting, "This one is softer than this one." She also showed interest in measuring which ones were heavier.

Serenity investigated the measuring tools on the table. Using her math skills, she counted on the measuring tape how long she wanted to cut her yarn.

Angelica felt the different textures and then chose one to work with. She connected it with her own identity: "I like this one. It looks like my hair."

We pondered how the identities of the materials could express our own identities. We offered the children a digital microscope in the hope that they would continue to connect the physical properties and attributes they discovered in the materials to their own features over the next few weeks.

Anita cut pieces of two different types of yarn and used the eyedropper to pour water over them. She observed, "The yarn changed size." If she used more water, the yarn shrank. She then decided to place a dry piece of yarn under the digital microscope, "Looks like hair!"

Joseph, Julian, and Greyson pulled apart the yarn to examine it further. Greyson observed, "The pink changed to red; looks like lava."

Shep placed yarn and fabric under the microscope and discovered how "the color changes" (referring to the yarn). He said, "It's dark, wow!" We discussed how our own hair can look darker when it's wet as well.

The children then pivoted. We thought they would use the materials to enhance their self-portraits by adding a three-dimensional element, such as using the yarn to represent their hair. However,

instead the children decided to use the fabrics to make clothing. This led us into a conversation about how our attire is an example of our self-expression. It is another means for sharing our identity.

With the revisiting journey taking this new turn, we spent time in our weekly community of practice exploring the different textiles, the sewing machine, and tools for sewing and weaving. Playing with materials inspired us and deepened our understanding of the affordances the various materials and tools offered children. We wondered what connections the children would make to their own interests and inquiries. We couldn't wait to see how these new materials would engage children in a different revisiting journey.

Reflective Questions

- How will you create opportunities for children to explore and revisit their identity in multiple ways?
- As an educator, what do you need to know to better support children's identity development?
- How will you engage children in conversations about differences and similarities?
- What art tools and materials can you incorporate into the ecosystem to explore identity?
- How might technology, such as projections, help support children's identity development?

CHAPTER 11

Learning Through Power

A Journey Through Fire into Shelter

In this chapter, the educators of Boulder Journey School tell their own story of a multiyear study of how children learn through power. Boulder Journey School is a full-day, year-round school for early childhood education and teacher education located in Boulder, Colorado. It welcomes approximately two hundred children, ages birth through five, and their families to learn alongside its faculty, which includes both full-time mentor teachers and resident teachers, who teach at Boulder Journey School for twelve months through its master of arts licensure residency program in partnership with University of Colorado Denver. All the work shared in this chapter was developed in collaboration with children, teachers, and families and with pedagogical support from the community.

Boulder Journey School recognizes the child's right to engage in experiences that are shaped and fostered by responsive relationships with the world around them. It prioritizes relationships to make it possible to uncover ever-increasing complexity through the children's questions and understandings within an unscripted process of contextual curriculum. In the journey explored in this chapter, mentor teacher Kirsten Zimbelman had the privilege to research alongside one group of children for all of their time at the school. Each year new coteachers and new classrooms added perspectives to the deep relationships that developed through the constant of Kirsten and the children. We began this examination two years into their work together and followed through their graduation from Boulder Journey School.

The parallel journeys in this chapter show the commitment of educators, children, families, and the pedagogical leads as they engaged in deep reflection and research to support the ongoing interest of the children.

A Three-Year Study of Power

In May 2020, when Boulder Journey School returned to in-person learning following a two-month shutdown due to the COVID-19 pandemic, Kirsten and the toddlers of room 9 returned to an emotional landscape that had been drastically altered. Teachers were afraid of the ease with which illness could spread inside a closed classroom. Families were afraid of the quality of the outside air following a massive wildfire in the local community. Everyone was afraid as the social and political unrest mounted in the wider global community. The children's play reflected this atmosphere, and their courage to explore these feelings inspired us to emphasize a strong image of the child that we as adults could learn from. Over the course of the following three years, we observed how this landscape shaped the experiences this class gravitated toward.

Year One: Exploring the Concept of "Scary"

Threads of fire and firefighters arose in play. The children turned buckets into helmets and rubber ramps into hoses. Inspired by these repurposed interpretations, the teachers shone a digital projection of a fire onto a blank space in the classroom. Dillon cried out, "There's a fire in the cube! It's not working, we have to spray faster!" Broc responded, "We have to spray it out!"

To extend the exploration of fire, we offered images of fires and videos of the children's dramatic play alongside red, orange, yellow, and brown colored pencils. Each classroom in our school contained a ministudio where children had consistent access to mark-making materials. We intentionally curated palettes of materials to offer as a thought provocation.

Both Dillon and Nico recalled the vivid colors of the fire:

Dillon: "When the wildfires were in the air, there was smoke. I'm trying to remember what it looked like. The fire burned and then there was smoke."

Nico: "This is what yellow fire looks like."

Dillon: "Orange is the wildfire color."

Parallel Journey

Revisiting the fire through mark making offered space for the children to process the experiences on a new level. The language of the marks invited personal

Dillon and Charlotte extinguish a projected fire using hoses constructed from large loose parts.

remembrances of being surrounded by smoke-filled air. We recognized that for children (and adults), fear is most often rooted in the unknown. It is through developing relationships with unfamiliar concepts that we move into a state of equilibrium.

In "The Pedagogy of Listening," Carlina Rinaldi (2011, 234) writes, "For both adults and children, understanding means being able to develop an interpretive theory, a narrative that gives meaning to the world around them." She goes on to highlight the importance of uncovering understanding through social context: "Expressing our theories to others transforms a world not intrinsically ours into something shared. Sharing theories is a response to uncertainty."

As the children engaged with the scariness of fire, we noticed they were also investigating more and more other things that made them feel scared. This represented a pivoting point in the children's interest and adult observations, and it was time for us to revisit and reflect as we realized that while the topic of our research had thus far been fire, the concept under investigation was scariness. When we stepped back and identified a concept instead of a more surface-level topic, we were able to open multiple new possibilities for exploration and offer experiences that provoked questions and theories that offered additional layers of understanding around the concept.

Trips to our school garden meant regular encounters with spiders. Spiders tend to cause unease in people. We observed displays of fear or reserved fascination as the children asked questions like "Why do spiders move the way they do?" "Why

Teagan and Dahlia build the web from the inside out.

do they eat bugs?" And "Why do they make webs?" We wanted to offer children an opportunity to develop their relationships with spiders through expanding their theories. We strung tape throughout the classroom to make a web, choosing tape rather than string to mimic the stickiness of spiderwebs.

As we wound tape into various spiderweb formations, the children moved their bodies through the web without getting caught and "turning into a fly." The children were embodying the spiders. Through body language and play scripts, they were investigating the creatures that made them nervous by becoming them.

As the strands of tape stuck to their bodies, clothes, and hair, and consequently broke in response to their movements, Dillon reflected, "In a real spiderweb, flies get stuck and break the web and then the spiders have to fix it."

Redding responded, "We have to be careful!"

Teagan, Story, and Callie pretended they were princesses trapped by a mean spider. "We can't get out! We are trapped!" wailed Teagan dramatically.

"The web is so sticky, it catches my hair. We will never get away!" agreed Story. The two defeated princesses then lay down and "cried" in despair.

Callie sat in the middle of the web and called out, "My boat is stuck in the spider shark web! Save me!" Callie's cry explored the feeling of vulnerability while also providing an avenue to engage her peers and invite them into her play.

As in the fire exploration, we invited engagement with spiders through the language of drawing. As Teagan worked, she narrated her thoughts about spiders, sharing, "The spiders are pulling this bug into the spiderweb to eat. Spiders are not scary. They are just hungry."

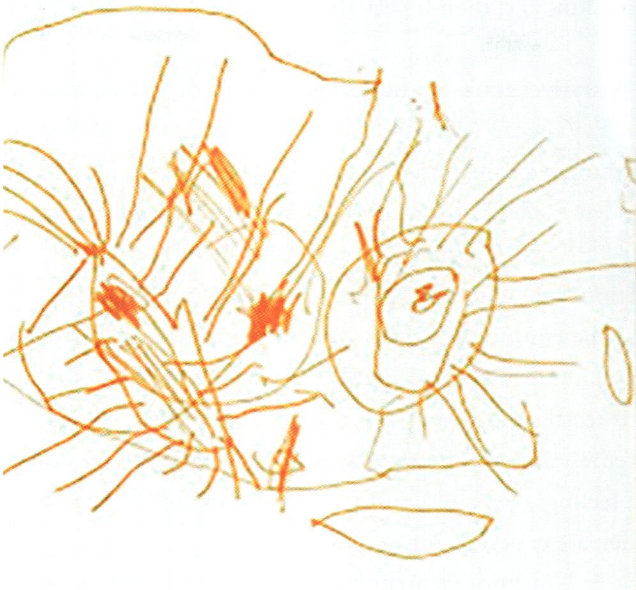

Teagan, a child two and a half years old, draws a spider.

Parallel Journey

Teagan's drawing and musings felt important. Teagan was demonstrating a move from assumptive thinking (that spiders are scary or mean) to dialectical thinking (that spiders are capable of violence and they act that way as a means to survive).

To go deeper within this line of thinking, we cultivated a classroom library tailored to the questions the children asked through their play, including stories such as "The Three Little Pigs," "Jack and the Beanstalk," and *The Paper Bag Princess* by Robert Munsch—all stories that include a big, bad character and acts of heroism. These characters, like the spiders and the fire, invited new pathways through which we could examine the concept of scariness.

Evy, age two and a half, depicts a scary monster and a sad whale.

We noted that the children were using the process of representing through languages such as drawing and clay to construct narratives that would help them navigate big feelings in their personal lives. Following a period of preventative quarantine for the class, Olivia talked softly to herself as she drew. She said, "The monster is sick because it has a thorn on its nose. The thorn makes it get a virus. To get better, the monster has to sniff the rose. The smell goes into its skin, and then it gets all better and doesn't have the virus anymore."

Sometimes the children's narratives took on the perspectives of the characters who were in danger, such as in Evy's representation. "This is a monster with wings," she explained. "This is a scary monster. The monster is scaring the whale. Those are its sharp teeth. It's going to eat the whale, so the whale isn't happy. It's sad it's getting eated."

Sometimes the representations included the perspective of the scary character. As Charlotte drew, she considered the emotions of the ogre in "Jack and the Beanstalk": "This is a picture of the ogre when he's mad. This part is the beanstalk. This is the top of the beanstalk. I drew his teeth inside there, but his mouth is closed, so you can't see them." This kind of representation offers a platform for developing radical empathy. By identifying these feelings, the children form fuller pictures of the characters. They are not "evil"—they are experiencing an emotion.

In the TED talk "Empathy Is Not Endorsement," Dylan Marron (2018) says, "Empathizing with someone you profoundly disagree with does not suddenly compromise your own deeply held beliefs and endorse theirs. . . . It just means that I'm acknowledging the humanity of someone who was raised to think very differently from me." Through their representations, the children had a platform to strengthen their understanding that they will encounter many people and situations they do not agree with or like.

Recognizing the affordances of different materials, we offered the children clay alongside the storybooks. We noted the elements of scariness included in these representations, such as teeth and wings, as well as the children's strategies to make them less scary. Teagan noted, "I'm making the ogre. I don't want my ogre to have sharp teeth. Him's teeth all falled out." Was this Teagan's way of taking control of the situation?

Sometimes the children's solutions were magical, such as in Teagan's case; other times they were very practical. When asked how to keep themselves from danger, Evy replied that we could "run to our mommies and daddies," and Charlotte added, "We can hide."

Parallel Journey

We considered ways to intentionally engage dialectic perspectives with the stories. Remember Teagan and the spider? The children were letting us know that they were capable of holding perspectives that conflicted. We added a series of stories to our classroom that would offer counterperspectives.

The idea of counterstories is one we learned from studying critical race theory. Critical race theory scholars Daniel G. Solórzano and Tara J. Yosso

(2002, 32) define counterstorytelling as "a method of telling the stories of those people whose experiences are not often told (i.e., those on the margins of society). The counterstory is also a tool for exposing, analyzing, and challenging the majoritarian stories of racial privilege." We felt it was important to encourage the children to question the ways in which power operated in these stories and to use this strategy to complicate the narratives the children were exploring. Posing counterstories invited children to encounter different sets of beliefs and work through how to relate to the perspectives they do not connect with initially.

Charlotte (three years) depicts the ogre and Jack sharing a house so they both have resources.

We purchased several books that told "twisted" fairy tales, narrated by the "villain." In some of these stories, rather than broadening the complexity and embracing collectivist solutions, we noticed that the authors swapped out one villain for the other. We wondered how we could find a third space. We asked the children to reflect. Were the villains really mean? Was the ogre from "Jack and the Beanstalk" wrong to be mad at Jack? The children shared that the ogre loved his harp and his chickens and then Jack took his favorite things.

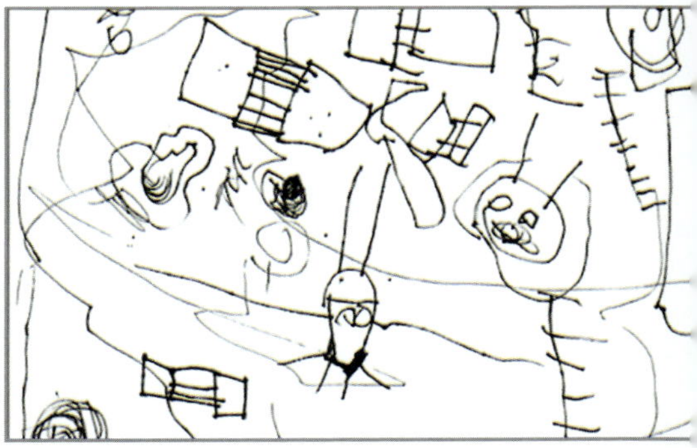

Evy (three years) also has a solution: Jack and the ogre working together to build and grow a vegetable garden.

Then we read a book that framed Jack as the villain. We engaged the children in conversations around this framing. The children recognized that Jack was hungry and came up with solutions to offer to Jack and the ogre that promote collectivism. They proposed that maybe instead of stealing each other's food, Jack and the ogre could build a community garden that they both could eat from. As the class moved into preschool, this relationship with radical empathy continued.

Year Two: Using the Hundred Languages

On December 30, 2021, a fire raged through Boulder County, destroying a thousand homes. While the Boulder Journey School community did not suffer any direct losses, every child was affected, whether they had been evacuated or simply felt fear and grief.

The children construct a house for bugs.

One sunny day in March, we stepped outside to play. We did not have a specific agenda: We were going out to enjoy the sunshine, breathe the fresh air, and move our bodies in big ways. We educators observed the children beginning a construction project. When asked, the children responded that they were building homes for the

Elias, three and a half years old, illustrates an underground bug house.

bugs who had lost their homes in the fires. This was the first time we understood fire as a platform for creation.

The children, making the connection between the construction site, the rebuilding of homes, and the bugs they had discussed, saw a pathway of possibility and took some steps down that road, inviting us to join.

Dillon: "We are making a house. It's a bug house."

Susie: "This is for the bugs that lost their house in the fire."

Educators: "What do you think bugs need or want for their house to be comfortable?"

Dillon: "They need flowers and mud, and a bed and a jar. We have the cone so the people know that it's a construction site."

Redding: "I brought more mud."

Educators: "What is the mud for?"

Redding: "The snow and mud is to help stick the house together."

This encounter generated energy that lasted beyond our afternoon outside. During our group gathering, the children's vision for the houses prompted brainstorming.

Elias: "We could go to the project playground and get some of the materials from there!"

James: "I'm making them a fence, so they have a yard. We also need a hive for the bees that lost their homes in the fire."

Elias: "I'm mixing this to get water for the bug house so they have some water."

Dillon: "All the wood chips look like the roof for the house. We've been working really hard to make this. We still have a lot of work to do."

Susie: "These boards could be the roof when we are done constructing. Then you can just walk across."

Again, mark-making materials acted as a language for extension of ideas. Blueprints became a basis for planning houses to accommodate different bugs.

Elias: "My bug house is underground because bugs like it underground. It has flowers and trees because they need those for nectar and a place to land. The sun has to be close so that it helps keep them warm."

Dahlia: "This is a spider house. It has lots of rooms to catch bugs and have spider sleepovers. That's the moon, and those are trees because they like those."

Parallel Journey

Reflecting on the powerful possibilities the children had dreamed of when adopting the perspective of the ogre the previous year, we recognized that the bug houses could offer another pivoting point that could potentially lead to a new revisiting journey to engage perspective taking. We observed the children simultaneously drawing from their own desires and their observations of bugs, as with the spider sleepover room. We valued this interweaving of perspectives and wanted to encourage the children to recognize when they were listening to others and when they were asserting their own wishes.

A new language we had been exploring would lend itself to this step of the journey. Earlier in the year, the classroom had acquired a single-lens reflex (SLR) camera. Our adult process of learning this new technology piqued the children's curiosity. Families donated old point-and-shoot cameras to work with, and children started developing fluency in the language of photography. Many were drawn to using photographs to show perspectives other than their own.

Elias, three and a half years old, illustrates an underground bug house.

Outfitted with cameras, a small group of children searched high up in the branches of the pine trees and down low among leaf litter and gravel on the ground, capturing photographs of abandoned spiderwebs and empty holes. The children considered which bugs might choose particular spaces for homes, and an overarching theme of safety arose as they thought about locations that were hard to access while also having proximity to resources such as food, water, and comfort.

Educators: "What do bugs need?"

Broc: "Water, because they die without water. Pollen—they need to eat!"

Susie: "And flies."

Naomi: "They need sleep."

Susie: "A pillow."

Lookouts are added to most future renditions of bug houses.

Elias: "Rain."

Susie: "But not spiders, because they fall down."

Broc: "Worms dry up. They need the rain."

Naomi: "Yeah, but when they die, they feed the ants."

Broc: "They dry up in a little pack so the ants can eat them. So bugs need other bugs."

Callie brought up the idea of bug houses needing a lookout, "to see if any predators are coming." Dillon expanded on this idea, adding two sticks to his clay structure. "Right here, these two sticks are antennas. They're on the radar." We invited the children to use clay to represent their ideas of bug houses.

One morning, the children arrived at school to find the light table covered with dried flowers and materials harvested from an open space nearby. James gathered cardboard tubes and taped them together in a pattern similar to a honeycomb. He remarked that this looked like a beehive and added pine cones and dried flowers into the holes to feed the bugs and keep them comfortable. He was concerned his classmates would step on his bug house, so he created a wall of blocks around it and added a sign saying, "Please don't break my bug house. We're in here."

James's house heavily centered protection, while others had features similar to those we see in our own homes, such as drainpipes, toilets, bedrooms, and play structures to keep the bug children happy. "There's a lot of dried flowers with pokies they can climb on," Dillon noted.

The more familiarity the children gained with the lives and perceived feelings of the bugs, the more they embraced bugs as cohabitants of their world. A familiar game of transforming us all into bugs developed. One morning, as we were a colony of ants, we constructed a house that had shade, a lookout spot, safety from rain and wind, and access to food and water—and was open to all bugs.

We prompted the children to think deeply about whether all bugs would want to live together. Elias shared, "We wouldn't want spiders and bees to live together because bees would get catched by the spiders, and the spiders would get stinged by the bee. So they wouldn't be safe."

Susie added, "We should not put spiders next to a beehive or an anthill because the bees and ants would all get catched. That means they aren't safe."

The children decided that they would build a house that was for everyone but spiders. They would build a separate house for spiders.

Parallel Journey

The more time we spent investigating bugs through multiple languages, the more nuance was woven into children's understanding of the perspectives of bugs. In the past, the children had made it clear that all bugs were welcome in their houses. The children were now musing about what that actually meant for the safety of the bugs living in the house. They realized that not all insects can live together easily. They did not exclude the spiders out of malice. Instead, as they had done with "Jack and the Beanstalk," they considered how they could apply design in a way that met the needs of all community members.

All these conversations included opportunities to extend the children's thinking from bugs to humans and to consider questions around societal needs that support an expansion from an individual perspective to a collective perspective. Throughout the work, we asked questions such as the following:

- Do bugs and humans need the same things?
- Are there basic needs for all living creatures that are important to survival?
- Should both humans and bugs be supported in the need for basic survival requirements?
- How do your needs differ from mine?

As we moved into the next school year, we found opportunities to apply these understandings to the humans in our community.

Year Three: Collaborating with Infants

As we began the fall 2023 semester, the beginning of prekindergarten for this class, our school set a goal of holding school-wide research topics. Each class would use one of two lenses, "The Natural World" or "Me, You, Us, We," to interpret the classroom research and contribute new ideas and understandings to community definitions. The children and educators in our class together selected "Me, You, Us, We," a study of identity.

Loris Malaguzzi (1993, 10), founder of the Reggio Emilia approach, said, "Among the goals of our approach is to strengthen each child's sense of identity through recognition by peers and adults." This journey of relationships—internal relationship with the self; external relationships with families, peers, and teachers; delicate relationships with the world around us—is critical work in early childhood. How does the individual help form the culture of a place? How does the community shape the identity of the individual?

For this class, the first steps in considering the concept "Me, You, Us, We" involved understanding the children's definition of community. At the beginning of the year, the class dynamic shifted as multiple classroom

Dahlia and Oliver adjust their body language to match the infant's.

communities merged to become one large community of room 11. We prompted the children to explore their understandings of the agreements held in different communities.

Callie: "Community is a big place where lots of people share it."

James: "Community is important because it means that everyone has a job to do."

Dillon: "Community is when lots of people work together to pick up trash. It means there is always someone who can help."

Children from prekindergarten observe Louisa's fascination with wire dangling in the hallway.

The children recognized that one's role may be different depending on which community one is participating in at the moment. Within their own classroom, the children ebb and flow through leading, following, observing, narrating, and so on. However, within the context of the school community, they are looked to as leaders based on age and experience.

Susie wondered what her role might feel like if she were in a class with Sonny, her younger brother in the infant room. We reached out to Sonny's teacher, who was excited for the possibilities of collaboration and invited the children of room 11 to help design box forts as part of the research the infants had been engaged in. We enthusiastically accepted this invitation and immediately started researching box forts. Quickly, however, we hit a stumbling block.

As we were discussing the possibility of adding a mailbox, Theo asked, "Do the infants want a mailbox?" Everyone stopped. How do we know what kind of box fort they want? Would it make more sense to begin with understanding the infants?

We arranged a meeting with the infants in the hallway. As the infants played, the older children observed and documented to make note of what the infants might like. In this first meeting, there were seven children from room 11 and four infants from room 3.

After our first meeting with the infants, we discussed how different groups have different expectations for how to interact. Ollie noted that our arrival had been overwhelming for the infants. "We came in too big and tall and loud. We needed to be down and lower so we weren't so big. And quieter." We decided that in future meetings, the older children would keep to groups of four or fewer so the infants would not be overwhelmed.

As the children of room 11 looked through documentation they had gathered, they considered how to listen to the infants' preverbal communication. The infants spent a significant amount of time playing with wire that was fastened to the railing in the hallway. Did this mean they liked the way the materials dangled and wiggled? We visited the materials room to find just the right elements for a gift.

Near the front of the materials room was a donation of adhesive gift-wrapping bows. Teagan, Susie, and Dahlia were drawn to these bows: They were shiny and sparkly and pretty, and they were not so small that they would be a choking hazard. They seemed perfect for the infants.

Parallel Journey

Inwardly, we pondered the way in which the children chose the bows based on their personal interest. Was it OK to gift something because the giver liked it? In his book *IntraConnected,* Daniel J. Siegel (2023, 59) discusses the ideal of integration, "honoring both differentiation and linkage, cultivating and combining both the inner identity of me and the inter identity of we as an intraconnected, integrative identity of Mwe."

While we strongly value centering the collective, we do not want to eliminate the self. Without the individual, we lose the drive for creativity and innovation. We lose the diversity of perspectives. We become a drearily homogenous group.

Teagan, Susie, and Dahlia had their lifetimes of experiences to guide them. They knew which things were fun. They really wanted to work with the bows and offer their joy to the infants. We can put our own spin on an interaction—we can offer our opinions and our gifts—and still remain open to feedback from our collaborators.

Soon the older children were ready to bring their gifts of wires and bows and present them to the infants. The infants were very excited to welcome the older children into the room and immediately pulled on the wires just as they had in the hallway. The older children had also attached some hard PVC tubes together as noisemakers. Felix, ten months, was drawn to the noisemakers and searched them out within the gift. He delighted in clacking the tubes together to hear the sound they made. A bell was attached near the tubes, so with each clack, the bell would jingle. Seeing the babies work with the bows was also gratifying and inspiring!

Claire and Oliver observe the infant exploring their gift.

Carefully constructing the box fort.

This time, as we revisited documentation back in our classroom, more questions arose: What was the infants' favorite color? Favorite shape? Teacher Charlotte set up a color provocation for the children. She arranged materials of many colors and documented the infants using them.

Room 11 decided the best way to figure out the babies' favorite color was to tally the number of times an infant held a particular color in each of the photographs. Looking at the documentation helped us determine that yellow was a popular color for the children of room 3.

Again, we journeyed to the materials room, this time with more information to guide the search. The prekindergarten children were able to use more of what they knew about their younger friends to create a second offering.

The preschoolers chose a big yellow ball because they had noted how many balls the infants had in their room. Rubber bracelets were another exciting choice, both because they were stretchy and because they seemed like a pleasant texture for chewing. Remembering Felix's love of clacking, the children placed clicky-clacky materials next to one another. Room 11 also showed their personalities by adding paintings and drawings to the gift.

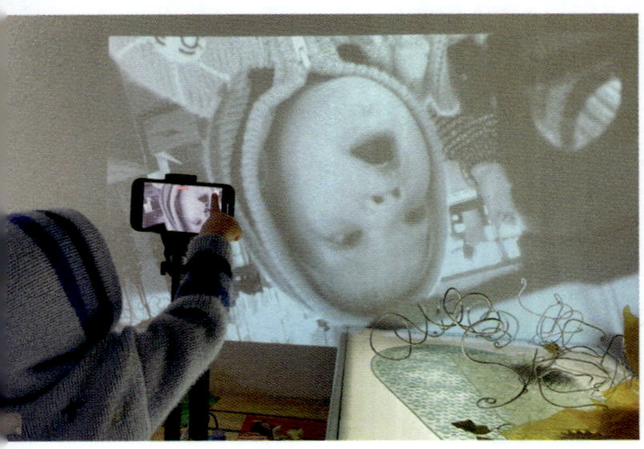

Exploring the features of the new box fort.

Following this experience, we determined we were ready for a first attempt at building a box fort. We returned to photos of the infants with their boxes and sketched our initial ideas. The ideas were elaborate! "We need multiple floors!" "They need an upstairs and a downstairs!"

To get a feel for the construction process, educators offered opportunities to begin on a small scale by creating tabletop box forts. Cardboard is tricky to work with, so our intention was to establish the affordances of the cardboard. What could it do? What could it not do? We realized that we needed to tape the edges of the cardboard because they were sharp and gave the children owies. We did not want that to happen to the infants. We added photos of the prekindergarten children and the infants to give a sense of scale—and to add a bit of delight.

We created an inventory of the boxes we had collected and considered box availability as a factor in our design. We also planned for elements we had observed the infants enjoying, such as peekaboo windows, working door flaps, and tunnels.

As we worked, Redding shared that box forts are fun "because it's a spot I can hide in and feel safe." This reminder of safety prompted the group to add windows so the teachers could see in. During the box fort building process,

Callie had a realization: "Are these windows too tall for the babies?" Discussion ensued. How could we measure to be sure? Should we bring a box to the babies? Should they come here so we could measure them next to the box?

The infants gather to explore the new box truck.

In the end, the children decided to go to the materials room to find something to help measure. The children found long strips of cardboard they could take to the infant classroom to mark each infant's height. Then we could bring the strips back to our classroom and use them to check the placement of the windows. Upon our return, we anxiously compared the measurements.

Following final touches of beauty (rainbow tape and drawings), we delivered the box fort to room 3. Two weeks later, we received documentation about the use of the box fort. One of the images showed infants Sonny, Felix, and Louisa playing in a medium-sized box. One child was pushing the box while the others took a ride in it. In the prekindergarten room, Dillon was very excited with this development. "Maybe we could make them a car," he exclaimed, "and a truck! And an airplane! And a garage!" Dillon had plans to make a whole fleet.

The room 11 children examined the boxes they had left over and decided to make a truck. They headed to the materials room to find anything that spoke to their intention of creating a truck. We were delighted when we found a real license plate to attach. Some materials were less literal. Bowls became headlights, and a piece of mesh packaging became a grill.

The room 11 children loved the new box truck. In a moment of deep play, Redding suggested, "I don't think this is big enough for the babies. We should just keep it." Despite this attachment, room 11 did deliver the truck to the children of room 3.

Parallel Journey

In meetings with infant teachers Charlotte and Jenelle, along with studio specialist Jacie Engel, Kirsten and Alex collaboratively developed the following reflection:

"The children's ideas were grand!" The teachers considered the balance between dreaming big and finding realistic possibilities. Dillon was determined to find a way to use real wheels and axles so the cardboard vehicle could roll. We knew this was an improbable dream, but we chose not to say that. While he suggested acquiring real wheels off the playground, Dillon eventually came to the challenge of how to attach them safely and happily modified his plans, delighting in the way old vinyl records looked glued into the space where a wheel well might be.

What a gift it is to have a part of the population who can dream so big beyond logistics. Freed from the fear of being shamed for being wrong or the anxiety around doing something "correctly," our minds will have no limits. So often, it is the adult mind that shuts down possibility. Educator Akeia Gross (2024) reminds us of the power of the child's mind. In seeking liberatory learning, they invite young children to dream of what a society that practices liberation could look like. Without the constraints of knowing what does and does not exist, children can bring to life what could exist.

We reflected on the power of dreaming big and bringing only parts of the dream to fruition. To dismantle our adherence to perfectionism, we intentionally engage in experiences that carry on even when the journey will not reach our idealized endpoint. This is how we bring about change—even if it begins as incremental change. We keep moving and avoid stagnation.

Something happens when we work on a creative endeavor; it starts to gain its own life. It develops its own self-propelling momentum, and we reach a point where it becomes clear it is going to happen. We are on a trajectory, a course that cannot stop. How amazing it is that we create these things, these ideas, that start to live!

This is much like the way our identities develop. Rarely, if ever, do we become exactly the people we thought we would be. And in our beautiful complexity, we can hold oppositional ideas as true simultaneously. We can mourn the idealism that has not come to fruition as we celebrate that it existed in any form.

What is significant to one member of the community does not have to hold the same significance for all members of the group, and there is space for us each to have our own relationship with an experience. Infant teachers Charlotte and Jenelle reflected that while the infants enjoyed the gifts that the older children made for them, they were not attached to the idea that these new creations were gifts, and certainly not that they were gifts from another class. The infants do not necessarily have the same connection to the process of gift making and giving that older children have. To infants, there is no difference between the items teachers offer and the gifts from older children. The infant teachers reflected that because the gift integrated so seamlessly that the infants could not tell the difference, clearly the older children had figured out what the infants would like.

We considered that this particular group of children have a worldview that is unparalleled. They came into the height of their social experimentation as the world shut down. They returned to school amid fear from so many angles: wildfires, illness, and strong social unrest. Their world has been one of upheaval, and yet they are responding by creating worlds of flexibility, adaptability, and stability for others.

Are the forts the children's way of designing their dreams of a world without the rigid and narrow thinking that currently prevails?

Viewing the children in relationship with their wider community offered a strong reminder that we are more than who we are individually; we are who we are in relation to those around us. Our identities are shaped in infinite ways based on our countless and ever-evolving relationships with the world around us.

Different contexts support different competencies. The relationships with the younger children offered views into the identities of the prekindergarten children of room 11 that had not been noticed before. What competencies are we not seeing because children have not found the right context in which to use them?

This is why it is so crucial to hold a strong image of the child. We have to trust that the child is competent even if the context they exist in stifles the presentation of their full competence. We have to be open to meeting the different versions of the child that exist in their core being and are still growing and blossoming. And what a gift this is to ourselves as well! Holding this image of the child means we must hold this image of ourselves. We are still allowed to grow and be whoever we truly are.

Reflective Questions

- **What do you need to change in your current program to allow for long revisiting journeys?**
- **How could you adjust the daily schedule to allow for revisiting and longitudinal work?**
- **What strategies do you need to record, analyze, and support a long-term revisiting journey?**
- **How could you reframe and rephrase daily practices and inquiries to support long-term revisiting journeys?**
- **How might you create a culture of inquiry, wonder, and curiosity that will maintain a long-term revisiting journey?**
- **How will you incorporate the concept of radical empathy in your practices?**

CHAPTER 12

Learning Through Nature

A Journey with Birds

The William Paterson University Child Development Center is located on the university's campus in Wayne, New Jersey. The center is a program of the university's College of Education and serves as a laboratory site for faculty, undergraduate, and graduate student research and coursework. It also provides a place for students to fulfill their clinical experience and student teaching requirements.

The five-classroom Child Development Center provides opportunities for children ages two and a half to six years old. The multilingual, multiethnic population includes children of William Paterson University employees, alumni, and neighbors. The center's philosophy of education incorporates the underpinnings of the Reggio Emilia approach to learning. The highly skilled teaching staff individualizes the program to encompass the unique developmental levels of children and recognizes differences in children's learning approaches. Provocations and investigations come from children's interests, and together with the educator, they coconstruct new learnings while exploring their topics and questions, testing their hypotheses and theories in meaningful, developmentally appropriate ways.

In this chapter, educator Lauren shares her valuable experiences while guiding preschool children through a yearlong exploration of the local flora and fauna, specifically focusing on the birds that live in their community. Throughout this journey, she actively researches and discovers innovative methods, tools, and materials to engage the children's interests and ideas, fostering a rich learning environment. Her parallel journey entries, written in the first person, not only demonstrate her reflective abilities but also highlight the profound impact of her methods on the children's learning and development. Lauren's parallel journey is an introspective conversation with herself.

We Found a Feather

On one of our daily hikes, the three- and four-year-old preschool children discovered a feather. They gathered in a circle and excitedly discussed it.

Artemis: "It's not from a peacock."

Matthew: "I think it came from an eagle or maybe a hawk."

Warren (three years old) and Ty (four years old) notice a V-formation while on a hike.

It became apparent that the children had an interest in investigating the feather.

Teacher: "I wonder how we might investigate which birds live near our school."

Warren: "I think we should google it, and then we can look at their feathers and see which bird this one came from.

As soon as we returned to the classroom, the children retrieved electronic tablets, and we researched northern New Jersey birds. Matthew, Tucker, Daniela, Artemis, Ty, Warren, Magdalena, and Mariah looked on as we scrolled through images of cardinals, blue jays, mourning doves, turkey vultures, and various finches, sparrows, woodpeckers, geese, ducks, and hawks. They asked, "What's this one called?" and declared, "That one's my favorite because I like [blue, red, yellow, stripes, spots, and so on]!" The children ultimately determined that more research was needed to identify the origin of the feather.

During our hike the next day, the children looked upward more than ever before, searching for birds. Warren and Ty shouted, "Look at the birds!"

Ty: "Maybe one of those birds dropped the feather we found."

Warren: "You see them flying up there? It kind of looks like a *V*."

Parallel Journey

I have felt a bond with nature as far back as I can recall. My mother was a biology teacher and seemed to be an encyclopedia of biophilia-related knowledge. Once I was about eight years old, her response to my questions became "Look it up." I would roll my eyes and walk over to the vast expanse of *Encyclopaedia Britannica* volumes and tirelessly search for answers. In hindsight, that process prepared me for handling a group of children who mass-produce questions like machines. It was surprising how much knowledge about nature I retained from childhood; I could often provide an answer. However, to make the children part of the research process, I would invite them to research examples to offer visual support. For example, when Warren described the formation of migrating geese as resembling a *V*, I validated his observation by introducing the term *V-formation*.

Exploring the V-Formation

When we were back in the classroom, I turned on the voice-to-text feature on a tablet and pulled up the search engine. Being familiar with this process from past investigations, Artemis said, "Show me the V-formation." As we scrolled through pictures, I realized that I could not recall why geese traveled that way. I asked the children to make some predictions. Tucker said, "Because that way they can stay together," and Warren said, "Maybe that's their favorite letter."

I asked, "If you were a migrating bird, what formation would you make?" He responded, "A W-formation for Warren."

Parallel Journey

That evening, motivated by the children's interest, I researched the scientific answer for why birds fly in a V-formation. I learned that birds use this formation mainly to reduce wind resistance. I immediately thought about my years running track and the strategy of drafting, or running behind someone to reduce wind resistance and conserve energy.

Considering wind resistance, I remembered a fan a colleague had given me as a humorous birthday present because, while others are wearing sweaters, I am constantly too hot from whipping around the room to match the children's energy. I retrieved the fan and set it up on top of a shelf at the height of the children's faces. I said, "Let's pretend to be birds in a V-formation and see if this formation really helps block the wind." The children lined up in their interpretation of a V-formation. Matthew was at the tip of the formation, directly in front of the fan. Then I asked, "Matthew, can you feel the wind?" He responded that it was "very windy." Then, I asked two children on either side and slightly behind him if they could feel the wind and they said, "Only a little." I asked the children why it wasn't very windy, and Tucker quickly responded, "Because they're standing behind Matthew, and he is blocking them from the wind." I asked the next two children if they felt the wind, and they said they could not. Before I could even ask why, Daniela excitedly said, "Because all of those people are in front of us, so we can't feel it!"

Based on our research, I learned that the bird in front of a V-formation will eventually travel to the back of the formation, and a well-rested bird will lead next and take on the majority of wind resistance. So I explained that if Matthew were a bird, he would get tired faster than the other birds because he was the one pushing against the wind the most. The children replied, "Oh, Matthew, you must be exhausted from pushing against the wind and blocking everyone else. You can go to the back of the formation and take a rest from the wind." The children decided to take turns leading the formation. I said, "Tucker, you look very well rested, would you like to lead the group?" He then stepped up, and we repeated the process, giving each child the experience of taking on the wind resistance.

After the children learned about the V-formation and learned why birds use it as a strategy to fly long distances, they became curious about the birds' destinations, which led to an investigation of migratory instincts. We revisited these ideas in the spring when we learned about homing instincts. Hearing the term *migration*, the children made an instant connection to a previous study involving monarch butterflies. "They're going to where it's warmer, like the monarchs do when they migrate to Mexico," said Tucker.

> ### *Parallel Journey*
>
> Exploring the migratory and homing instincts of birds fosters an understanding of directionality, distance, geography, and climate. In a previous study on mapmaking, some of the children had become familiar with compasses. After that, compasses remained in the science area because the children still used them when investigating magnets and during their dramatic play. Since investigations using a compass would help children conceptualize the directions that birds navigate during their migratory and homing journeys, I decided to access that prior knowledge.

Learning About the Compass

I asked the children how we could figure out which direction the birds were migrating. Matthew said, "We have to use a compass," and he went to the science center to get one. As the children gathered around, I asked, "Who can tell me which direction is north?" "You have to look for the arrow with the *N*," said Tucker. He analyzed the compass and confidently said, "It's that way," indicating the north direction. I then asked which way was east, and Artemis said, "That way, because I see the *E*." Intentionally leaving south for last, I asked which direction was west, and all the children pointed west as Mariah said, "The *W*." Before I could even ask, Matthew said, "And that's south. That's where the birds are going to get warmer, maybe like Mexico."

Daniela, Mariah, Artemis, Magdalena, Tucker, Matthew, and Ty using a compass to identify the direction south.

Mourning dove made by Mariah; Tucker creating a blue jay; Harper creating a pink bird; and Evan creating a hawk.

As the children continued investigating their compasses, Matthew said, "I'm going to make a bird that migrates." There was an uproar of "Me too!" as the children gathered materials and headed to different centers to begin creating interpretations of migratory birds. Mariah went straight to the clay area and began manipulating the clay into a head, body, and legs. I noticed her trying to pick up the clay bird only to have it fall apart. She reassembled her bird, then visited other centers to explore other materials, and ultimately she chose a tree round from the science area and transferred her bird onto it, pressing downward. Then she went to the Loose Parts area, carefully chose two seashells, and pushed them into the clay. She looked at me with an expression of accomplishment and said, "There! Now it has wings. Here is the head and this is the beak. The legs got squished, but he doesn't need them. He just needs his wings to migrate."

As the children continued to work on the birds, Tucker explained, "I made a blue jay. I gave it big wings so it can fly better when it's in front of the V-formation." Harper said, "Mine is a Harper bird. I made it pink because pink is my favorite color." Evan explained, "I'm using clips to make the wings stay."

Searching for places to display their bird sculptures, the children began collaborating.

Matthew: "My bird is so strong. I think he could lead a V-formation."

Tucker: "We should all make a big V together. I'll put mine next so when yours gets tired, my bird will move to the front."

Daniela: "I think my bird is already tired, because it took me a long time to make it. I'll put mine in the back so he can rest a little."

After the children lined up their birds into a V-formation, they asked me to hang them from the ceiling to look like they were flying. I asked what we should use to hang them, and Magdalena confidently went to the art center and brought back a spool of clear plastic string. Without hesitation, the children began cutting strings and experimenting with glue and tape, while others began tying knots around their birds. I also provided several paper clips and binder clips. Two children attached the string to their birds using binder clips, and two other children observed the successful strategy and duplicated it.

Based on the weight of some of the bird creations, I knew that tape would not be strong enough to attach them to the ceiling. I studied the ceiling and noticed what appeared to be strips of metal holding the ceiling tiles in place. I immediately thought about using magnets to connect the strings. To determine which parts were magnetic, I went into the office and got the circular magnets used in the trajectory wall in the hallway as they were stronger and I knew they would hold more weight than magnet clips.

I placed a chair in the middle of the room and said to the children, "I'm going to stand on this chair to see where we can use the magnets to hang our birds."

Knowing that the children were familiar with the term *magnetic* from a previous study, I invited them to help me investigate which parts of the ceiling were magnetic. I held the magnet in the center of a ceiling tile and let it drop into my other hand. "Magnetic?" I asked. "Not magnetic," Warren responded. Next, I tried part of the metal strip holding the ceiling tiles in place. But to my surprise, the strips were not magnetic. Each time I moved the chair and tried a new location, the children accurately shouted, "Not magnetic!" We burst into laughter because each place that I thought would be magnetic was not.

I asked, "Does anyone have any suggestions? Because I can't seem to find a part of the ceiling that's magnetic." At last we saw a vent in the center of the room. I asked the children if we had tried that place, and they confirmed that we had not. As I held the magnet up, it was forcefully pulled out of my hands and adhered to the metal with a loud sound. "Magnetic! We found it!" they all shouted in celebration.

I explained to the children that I had only three magnets. "That's not enough for all of our birds," informed Tucker. I could hear several children counting at once as Tucker confirmed, "No, that's not enough. We have eleven birds." I invited the children to help find a way to attach the birds to something that would keep them in order and be held using a single magnet. Daniela got a ruler and placed it along one side of the V-formation of birds and instantly said, "Nope, too short." "We need something much longer," said Artemis. Ty went to the block center, where we kept several large branches that the children had found over the school year. "How about this one?" he asked with a laugh, since it was nearly twice his size. "Let's try it," I suggested. "It's long enough, but it's going to be too heavy," advised Matthew. I noticed Mariah opening up one of the magnetic clips as wide as it would go and said, "The clip isn't big enough. We need a smaller stick." Ty, Matthew, and Warren went back to the block area and brought back two small sticks, lined them up next to the birds in the shape of a *V*, and declared them perfect.

I offered to help by tying loops at the end of the strings and explained that they would need to put the stick through the loops so the birds would stay in the order they chose. The children excitedly put the stick through the loops and then asked me to put the clip on and attach it to the ceiling. When they heard the loud thud of the magnet attracting to the vent, the children cheered and immediately began helping one another feed the second stick through the remaining loops. When I put

it up, I intentionally placed it parallel to the first stick. "How does it look?" I asked with a straight face. The immediate responses were laughter and shouts of "What?" "No!" and "You're just being silly!" "What's wrong with this?" I asked. "It has to make a point so it looks like a *V*," said Artemis. As I corrected it, the children confirmed, "Yes!" and "Like that." Then Matthew said, "Since my bird is first, I'm going to make a sign so they know which way is south. That way he won't get lost." Ty, Tucker, and Daniela followed and began making additional signs.

Above, signs created to help migrating birds identify south.

Tucker went to the science center to get the book on bird migration that was displayed with the compasses and proceeded to look for the word *south* to be sure it was spelled correctly. Ty wrote the letter *S* independently, and Matthew and Daniela wrote "Help for cold birds this way" and "Hot weather here," respectively, using invented spelling. I noticed that Daniela was working on her sign for quite a while. I asked her to tell me about the details she was adding, and she said, "I'm using this bird hole puncher, because if some birds can't read, then they will see all of these birds going south, and they will follow them to where it's hot." Tucker was the first to put up his sign, and the others added their signs near his.

The children revisited their creations in the spring, when they noticed unfamiliar birds on campus. First, Daniela observed Canada geese in the pond. "Look at that gaggle of geese! I think those are the same ones that we saw flying to Mexico a long time ago." "I think you're right," said Anthony, nodding in agreement. I added more information to the children's dialogue: "Those geese probably migrated back home to New Jersey. Migrating home is actually called *homing*. Why do you think they came back to New Jersey?"

Amelia: "Because they live here, and they had to come home from vacation."

Cody: "Maybe it got too hot so they came back."

Tucker: "They have to go north to come back here like the monarchs."

When we returned to the classroom, it was time for lunch, so I took the opportunity to revisit the book *Follow the Flyway* by Sarah Nelson. Then, using the tablet's talk-to-text feature to model how the children can do research with their families, I asked the search engine, "Why do birds return to New Jersey in the spring?" I read an explanation to the children, which informed them that migrating birds travel back north because they prefer the seeds from the plants here and the insects here are the best for baby birds.

During morning meeting the next day, we revisited the question of the day: "Which direction do birds travel when they are homing back to New Jersey?" Matthew immediately responded, "North!" I asked the children how we could identify which direction was north, and Artemis said, "Let's get the compass again and look for the *N* for north." She got the compass, and the children gathered in the center of the room and began to replicate the actions they had taken to identify the south in the fall, using that strategy to identify north.

Looking up at the V-formation above their heads, Matthew said, "My bird is going to lead the other birds back to New Jersey. We have to make them all turn around." I removed the sticks holding the V-formation and the children took them from my hands and, in unison, they turned them around. "We have to make new signs that say 'north,'" suggested Ty. "I'm going to make a sign that says 'home,'" said Mariah. Daniela, Tucker, and Matthew also made signs that said 'north.' The

children revisited the V-formation now coming north.

Feeding the Birds and Giving Them Shelter

Back in the late fall, as the weather became colder, the children had noticed that they could still hear birds on our hikes. "I still hear birds," said Warren. "Why didn't they go south with the other birds?" "Maybe because they like the cold like you, Ms. Lauren," suggested Artemis. Already familiar with resident birds from my childhood, I explained that these winter birds stay here for all the seasons. "Yeah," said Matthew, "They are foraging for food so they can have food to eat even when it's cold. I'm going to put out food for them at my house—maybe a lot of bird seeds." Building on that, I said, "I wonder how we can help feed the birds that live by our school. That might be a great way to observe and document these resident birds." "Can you get some bird seeds so I can make a bird feeder?" asked Ty. The rest of the children responded with "Me too."

Sloane (three years) using a North American bird guide to identify spring birds visiting our bird sanctuary.

Parallel Journey

That night, I researched New Jersey resident birds and found good photographs of each with transparent backgrounds. I put them into a document and resized them to scale, which I was able to do because I had been observing them since I was a child and knew their sizes. I cut them out and laminated them, put a piece of magnetic tape on the back of each, and planned to introduce a resident bird species for three days each over the next several weeks. The first day we would discuss the physical features of a species, the second day we would discover their eating preferences, and the third day would be dedicated to learning the bird's call.

I expected that observing the behaviors and feeding habits of resident birds and their interactions with other species would ignite children's curiosity about what drives a bird's habitat preferences. As children wonder, they formulate hypotheses and engage in investigations to find answers. Observing resident birds would foster identification skills as children took note of the birds' physical characteristics and bird calls. This knowledge would arm children with details and allow them to form both symbolic and realistic representations of bird species through art, dramatic play, and the exploration of sound. I also expected that as their abilities to identify birds became more refined, the children would organize their information to represent their observations and aggregate data to reflect their findings and form inferences.

Sloane, Harper, Magdalena, Juan, Tucker, and Amelia investigating a feather found on the way to a hike.

During morning meeting, the children were discussing ways resident birds might find shelter during the winter months. I asked the children where they might seek shelter from the cold if they were birds. Unanimously, the children said, "In a house." The question of the day became "How might we provide shelter for our resident birds?" Matthew responded, "We need wood to build a house." Ty added, "And nails and a hammer to hold it together." "Maybe glue too," suggested Sloane. As the children named materials, I wrote down their list.

Parallel Journey

As the children were enthusiastically listing materials, I had flashbacks of woodworking with my father when I was a child. I remember him teaching me to use his tools and even making extra holes in a tool belt so that it would fit around my four-year-old waist. I felt so proud as the tools hung down past my knees. I was excited to be using his equipment. I recalled how he introduced each tool, demonstrated how it worked, warned me of what not to do, and then gave me the opportunity to use the tool. I recalled feeling so empowered, and I could not wait to give the class the same experience.

I raided my father's toolshed, taking a saw, a hammer, screwdrivers, a power drill with bits, a Dremel, nails, screws, a level, a tape measure, protective eyewear, and pieces of scrap wood. Looking at the array of tools, I thought about the three-year-old children in my class and knew that the tools would be too heavy for them. So, I postponed introducing tools to the children until I had authentic child-sized tools, which I immediately ordered for an overnight delivery.

I established a woodworking station in the classroom and introduced the child-sized tools during morning meetings over a few days. From my own

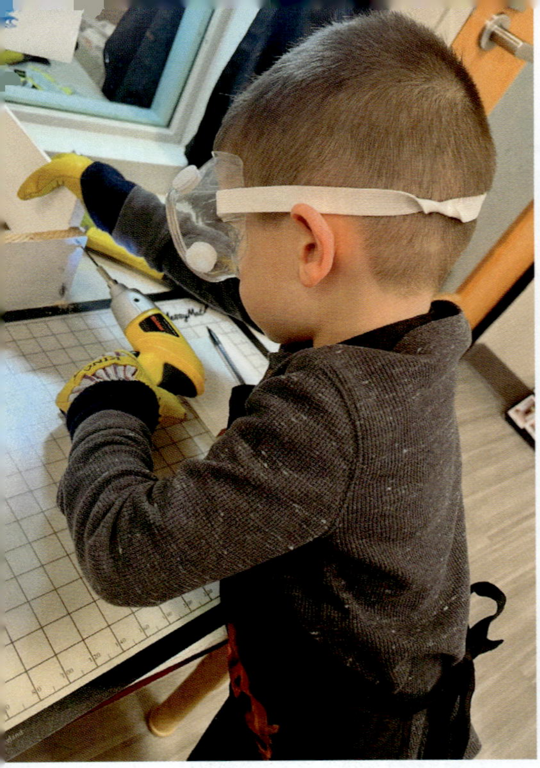

Matthew (four years) woodworking using a power drill.

Tucker (four years) woodworking using a hacksaw.

Space outside our classroom (November 2023).

experience, I knew that woodworking with authentic tools made the zone of proximal development easily recognizable, thus providing opportunities for scaffolding that would lead to autonomy and ultimately a greater sense of accomplishment and ownership (Vygotsky et al. 1978). Additionally, woodworking supports the development of mathematical skills such as measuring, counting, and comparing sizes, which offer a hands-on opportunity to develop an understanding of concepts such as height, length, width, and volume. When the children became curious about birdhouses, they were influenced by their empathy for the birds they observed. Their desire to provide a safe place to inhabit required critical-thinking and problem-solving skills to ensure that their structures were stable and functional. By using reclaimed wood and recycled materials, children learned about the importance of sustainability, environmental responsibility, and conservation.

The children created and fine-tuned blueprints, identifying which tools they would need to construct their ideas. When the children had their turns using the tools, I did exactly as my father had done: I described the tool, demonstrated how it is used, described what not to do, and then allowed the children the opportunity to use the tool.

Noticing that some children were hesitant at the sounds the drill made, I decided to provide my warnings in a way that would empower instead of frighten them. I offered clear instructions: "You need to rest your hand here to keep the drill straight, because if it comes out the side, it will hit my hand, and I will get hurt." Just as I had hoped, the children's safe use of the tools was driven by their desire to keep me safe instead of being fearful. As they were creating, I noticed that some of the younger children needed extra help when drilling and sawing through wood. I bought twelve-by-twelve pieces of thick corkboard for these children's use. With that adjustment, all the children were able to work with the tools they were curious about. They displayed their blueprints, and over time they redesigned and added structural and aesthetic details that made their creations closely resemble their plans. We always took protective measures. Even after they were working autonomously, I still stood next to them and watched intently to be sure they were being safe and responsible.

Next, the children thought of making bird feeders and placing them in a safe place. I asked the children what kind of food we should put in our feeders, and nearly all of them shouted, "Bird seeds!" I asked the children if birds eat anything else and received no responses. Ella said, "Just tell us!" I smiled and said, "I could, but what would you do if I weren't here?" Several children shouted, "Google it!" Using the talk-to-text feature, Ty asked, "What do woodpeckers eat?" The specificity of his question surprised me because, until that moment, the children hadn't seemed to have a particular species in mind. Ty found a picture of several insects and

Bird sanctuary with child-made bird feeders (January 2024).

a picture of a woodpecker retrieving some via the hole in the tree. He shared with the class, "Hey guys, they eat bugs that live in the trees. That's why they make that sound. It's 'cause they wanna get the bugs in there." After searching several pictures, he asked me to read the words in the article he chose based on the picture. As I read, we came across the term *suet.* Before I could finish the sentence, he asked, "What's suet?" I described it as "butter for birds mixed with bird seeds." As anticipated, Warren asked, "Can you get some for our bird feeders?" I responded, "I could, but wouldn't it be more fun to make it?" The children's eyes lit up.

The next day, I brought in a jar of sunflower butter, transferred several spoonfuls to a plastic container, and heated it in the microwave for a few seconds to soften it. I mixed it into a paste using craft sticks and placed it in the center of the table next to a bowl of bird seeds and a basket of unscripted materials. The children started off using craft sticks to spread the sunflower butter on their objects and sprinkled the bird seeds on them. I noticed Magdalena staring at her hands and analyzing how the seeds were sticking to certain parts. Daniela noticed and repeated one of our classroom mottos: "It's OK, we get messy in preschool!" This got Warren's attention, as he immediately put down his craft stick, scooped sunflower butter with his hands, dipped them right into the bird seeds, and pressed the mixture onto his tree round. Magdalena and Daniela proceeded to do the same. Once the children finished the bird feeders, we placed them outside on the window ledge and on the ground. Each day, the children observed the bird feeders they created. They made notes to keep track of what the birds ate. As a group, we revisited the data we collected and added more seeds or adjusted the location of the bird feeders as needed.

After noticing that wild turkeys had taken all the food from their ground bird feeders, some children chose to alter them to become hanging feeders. Children who noticed that their bird feeders were breaking from wind, precipitation, or the weight of perched birds reinforced their feeders with stronger strings and adhesives and added rocks to provide stability. Watching from the window, Ella said, "Hey, the birds are always eating from the other bird feeders and not mine." I said, "I wonder why." She stood for a moment and said, "Maybe it's because they have nowhere to sit. Can I go get it and put a ladder for them?" By the time she retrieved the bird feeder, Ella already had a plan for her revision. She placed the bird feeder on the art table and thoughtfully chose one of the larger craft sticks. She proceeded to attach it using tape and tested its durability by putting weight on the end of it. Each time it broke off, she added more tape until it finally withstood the pressure of her finger, and then she said, "Okay, I fixed it. Now we just have to put it outside and wait for birds." She patiently waited for three days until a pair of male and female house finches landed on it. "Look! The mommy and daddy house finches are both on my feeder! I did it!"

While learning to identify differences between males and females of a species and observing courtship behaviors, the children decided to provide a place where the females could wait for the males to bring them food. Reflecting on a book about starlings and how they congregate in trees, Juan said, "I think we need a roosting tree so the mommies can wait for the daddies to bring them food." Ty responded, "Oh yeah, I'm going to find a big one in the woods next time we go on a hike." I asked the children if they wanted to go on a hike and search for the perfect roosting tree, and they eagerly agreed.

As we went on our daily hike, I took a position as an observer. I listened to the children describe what they liked about some branches and the responses of others as to why a particular tree would not make an effective roosting tree. I was curious to listen to the children's ideas. Sloane found a small branch with several small twigs stemming off it and said, "How about this one? There's a lot of branches, so a lot of birds can sit on it." Matthew walked over and bent one of the twigs on Sloane's branch, and it instantly broke off. He explained, "This isn't a good one. These pieces are not strong enough. If a bird perches on it, it's going to break." Sloane briefly analyzed Matthew's rationale and swiftly accepted it. Ty noticed a large tree branch with several branchlets on the ground and began testing the strength of the branches just as Matthew had done. "This is a good one," he declared. "It's nice and strong. I think a big peregrine falcon can sit on this, and it still won't break." Tucker agreed: "Yeah, this way a whole family can roost on it." Matthew confidently walked over and repeated the same test he had done on Sloane's branch, and when it did not break, he agreed it was a good choice. The children immediately grabbed a piece of the large branch and began walking it back to the classroom without me advising or interfering. The children decided to create a bird sanctuary using the branch.

The children began noticing several species of birds appearing each day. Through their investigation into the identification of these varied species, the children realized that the previously migrating birds were now homing, and they wanted to research specific foods that would attract them. Their findings suggested that Baltimore orioles favor oranges and grape jelly, and they decided to place some in the roosting tree.

The Birds Need a Bath

After we read *Little Bird Takes a Bath* by Marisabina Russo, Sloane said, "I think our birds need a fountain like that to take a bath." The other children agreed, and Matthew decided to make a blueprint. When I asked what materials they needed, they said water and a big bowl. I asked the children if it was possible to make a bowl ourselves. "We could use clay," Juan suggested. "No, that would take too much clay. We need cement." To my surprise, the rest of the class appeared to know exactly what cement was and agreed.

Provocation for providing nesting materials to birds visiting the developing bird sanctuary.

Bird sanctuary with added nesting materials, trumpet vine, and sprouting wildflowers (May 2024).

Parallel Journey

Well aware that cement would be much too heavy to transport from the classroom to the bird sanctuary, I researched do-it-yourself birdbaths and chose a plaster that was safe for children. On the drive home, I brainstormed ways to give the birdbath shape, while still having the children as the decision-makers. I brought in a large bowl, a garbage can lid, and the metal cover from my firepit. I left them in my office where the children could not see and asked the children what we could use to make the birdbath shaped like Matthew's blueprint.

During a group gathering, I asked the children, "What can we use to make a birdbath?" The children looked around, and Warren said, "Everything is too small. We need a really, really big bowl." I went into the office and retrieved the large bowl and asked, "What do you think about this bowl?" The children were noticeably surprised at the size of it. Then Ty asked, "Do you have a bigger one?" I responded, "Maybe," with a smile,

Tucker, Ella, Matthew, Harper, Amelia, Ty, Ella, and Artemis planting and caring for native pollinator plants in the bird sanctuary (June 2024).

and I brought out the bowl-shaped garbage can lid. The children laughed, and Matthew said, "Bigger!" I went into the office and retrieved the firepit cover, and the children cheered and laughed. When I said that it was the biggest bowl I could find, they happily chose it for the mold.

I covered the table with a garbage bag to protect it from the plaster and make cleanup easier. Some children needed help putting on their gloves, but other than that, they were able to figure out what to do with the plaster without my guidance. After it dried, the children brought over the cart that we use to transport our materials for outdoor activities, and before we made it to the door, Juan said, "Wait! We need a bucket of water!" This made me laugh, because I had completely forgotten about water. I carried a bucket with several gallons of water, and the children rolled out the birdbath. Since the bird sanctuary is on top of a steep slope, I carried the birdbath up, and the children poured the water. The children welcomed the birds:

Amelia: "There you go, birds."

Harper: "Now you won't be dirty anymore."

Sloane: "And now you'll have water to drink too, because this is your safe habitat."

Warren: "It's your sanctuary."

As the children watched their birdbath for several days, reveling in their accomplishment, Ella asked, "What did that bird have in its mouth?" "I think maybe it was a worm," suggested Anthony. "No, it was green," she protested, "I think it was some grass." Overhearing this conversation, I retrieved the book *Robin's Home* by Jeannine Atkins, and since it was the end of the day, I read it after our daily reflection.

Instantly recognizing the connection to how birds build their nests, Ella said, "Hey! I saw a bird carrying that in its mouth today!" "Let's put some stuff out for that bird to use to make a nest," suggested Anthony. At that time, parents began walking in to pick up their children, so I suggested that the children might want to ask their parents to help research nesting materials that we could provide the birds.

Bird sanctuary (July 2024).

Parallel Journey

Taking my own advice, that night I researched nesting materials for New Jersey birds and noticed that an effective way to provide nesting materials is to create nesting balls. So as not to limit the children to ball-shaped creations, I trimmed forsythia and lilac branches from my yard because I knew that their branches were pliable and could be made into different shapes, thus making them unique to each creator. I proceeded to search the house, classroom, and office, gathering materials suggested by my research, such as cotton, moss, yarn, and twine, all the while feeling increasing anticipation to discover what the children might do with them. I also learned that providing dryer lint is no longer recommended because it can cause birds to choke. Before the children arrived the next morning, I had a table set up that displayed all the materials I'd collected the night before along with a sign with the question: "How might you use these to provide nesting materials for the wild birds?"

While planning for the end-of-the-year school event, when the children would share their learning about birds, the children began wondering if the visiting birds would have enough food when they were not present to replenish the bird seeds. Noticing that there was a thistle plant depicted on the bag of bird seeds we use, Ty suggested planting one near our bird sanctuary. Making a connection to a book about hummingbirds, Juan then suggested planting a trumpet vine to attract hummingbirds. Tucker suggested planting sunflowers because he had identified sunflower seeds in the wild bird seed mix we had been using for our bird feeders.

During our morning meeting the next day, I changed the question of the day to "Which plants provide food for birds?" Using the smartboard, we entered the question into a search engine, and each child had the opportunity to choose what they wanted to plant for our birds. Using the pictures found in this research as their guide, some of the plants the children chose were cosmos, aster, thistle, milkweed, sunflowers, trumpet vine, trumpet honeysuckle, Virginia creeper, and various colors of coneflowers. Soon the center's director purchased plants, seeds, gloves, rakes, and shovels of various sizes, and the children worked together to plant and care for the vegetation, which grew into a colorful flower garden for our bird sanctuary.

Parallel Journey

Caring for birds and their habitat fosters connection, empathy, and respect for living creatures. Creating a safe place for birds to have access to all their needs helps children understand the effects of human actions on wildlife and the importance of conservation and sustainability. By continuing to revisit the space, children were able to engage in long-term learning, allowing opportunities to adjust, improve, revise, and add to the space as they acquired new information. Developing and maintaining a bird sanctuary promotes preplanning and problem-solving skills and facilitates communication, collaboration, and teamwork.

Reflective Questions

- **What can you learn from your local natural ecosystem?**
- **How can you engage children to explore your local ecosystem, whether you live in a rural, suburban, or urban community?**
- **What resources do you need to support a revisiting journey of learning through nature?**
- **What knowledge do you need to support children's interest in nature?**
- **How can you introduce sustainability to young children?**

CHAPTER 13

Learning Through Story Making

A Yearlong Journey into Storytelling

The revisiting journey in this chapter illustrates how the educators of William Paterson University Child Development Center and its director, Cindy Gennarelli, guide children in a revisiting journey of learning through story making. The revisiting journey emerges from the children's ideas, interests, and hypotheses. The children and adults coconstruct new learnings while exploring their topics and questions, testing their hypotheses and theories in meaningful, developmentally appropriate ways as they meet the kindergarten standards. The educators' parallel journey entries, written in the first person by Cindy, highlight how kindergarten children demonstrate their knowledge of language and literacy (vocabulary, sequence, rhythm, comprehension, and using words in the correct context) as they integrate language and literacy into everyday practice. The parallel journey validates and clarifies how the revisiting journey framework can be applied in kindergarten.

We Are Story Makers

Children are natural storytellers, and they define their personhood and identities through their stories of wonder, playful inquiry, success, strengths, and capacities. Understanding the importance of this process and learning to carefully and

Children use their photographs to become characters in their stories while using a projector.

thoughtfully observe how children discover and make meaning of what they see can help us get to children's hearts and inner cores.

At William Paterson Child Development Center, the educators foster initiative and creativity among kindergarteners. At the start of the school year, educators develop an emergent curriculum that aligns with children's interests. Due to the transient nature of their preferences, identifying children's interests is a complex, dynamic, and continuous process. Daily observations allow me to record how children interact with their environment and how they enter into inquiry. An emergent curriculum also requires that I align the daily schedule to allow children the time they need to revisit their ideas. Incorporating the possibilities for revisiting their work meaningfully helps me collect anecdotes and chronicle their stories of discovery. Revisiting journeys promote individual expression without the constraints of a structured task yet allow me to record the essential learning outcomes required in kindergarten. The New Jersey Department of Education requires kindergarten environments and curriculum to be developmentally appropriate. The New Jersey kindergarten standards require that academic concepts be taught through project-based learning, a balance of child-initiated and teacher-guided learning that starts with a central idea and is studied over an extended period. I've found that the revisiting journey framework is fully aligned with this standard and enhances teacher-child interactions.

Parallel Journey

New Jersey kindergarten outcomes require educators to foster children's trust, security, and social development through warmth, caring, and responsiveness to individual children's interests and feelings. With these outcomes in mind, the teaching practice is focused on reflection supported by daily records of each child's actions, inquiries, and meaningful quotes. Keeping a copy of the lesson plan and taking detailed notes allows me to easily document and revisit each child's observations, wonders, interests, and strengths. This practice helps educators understand each child's unique abilities while identifying areas for growth. Educators can also identify many of the required kindergarten outcomes without having to directly teach the children.

Although educators collect daily holistic assessments, their reflective notes outline each child's unique journey. These records consist of informal written notes, photographs, and videos that capture their interactions with the environment and peers and their unexpected discoveries. By documenting these moments, educators can highlight the child's individual experiences, growth, learning, and development in a way that structured assessments alone cannot. In this process, I demonstrate that we meet the required outcomes while increasing children's inquiry and creativity.

The detailed anecdotes allowed educators to review children's growing interest in creating and telling their stories as they explored forest animals, designed toys, and built a boat. Their journey underscores the balance between creating opportunities for children to engage in collaborative projects and providing the space for individual exploration. While educators recognize the importance of fostering twenty-first-century skills such as collaboration, they also understand that academic knowledge is not just about textbooks and tests but happens in the context of social relationships. These relationships play a significant role in shaping a child's learning experience.

Planning how to challenge each child further is possible because of my observations and reflection. The New Jersey standards require educators to create an environment that promotes cognitive development by doing the following:

- incorporating daily planning and reflection times into the schedule
- ensuring easy access to classroom areas and materials that provide the backdrop for children's activities, projects, and plans
- using open-ended questions to encourage children's thinking
- observing children to learn about their interests, what they know, and what they are thinking about
- listening carefully to children's plans and the questions children ask to prepare appropriate supports
- encouraging children to describe in detail the outcomes of their plans
- encouraging children to use their outcomes as stepping stones to new plans
- making opportunities available for children to represent ongoing activities and projects through writing, drawing, and three-dimensional media

With the standards in mind, the educators have created an ecosystem that encourages play, collaboration, and ongoing reflection.

The Story Making Begins

The children eagerly embarked on yearlong storytelling journeys. It started with simple stories that became more elaborate over time. Throughout the year, we delved into the intricacies of crafting captivating tales. The educator facilitated this process by setting up daily invitations with a diverse range of unscripted materials carefully chosen to stimulate the children's imagination and support them in developing their oral stories.

Our proximity to a hiking trail sparked the children's interest in storytelling, which centered on forest animals. To support this interest, we provided a rich variety of unscripted materials, from natural elements like branches and twigs to everyday items like household tools, fabric samples, and bottle caps. This diverse range of materials, along with traditional ones like cardboard pieces and glass pebbles, was readily available and frequently rotated, providing a wealth of resources for the children's storytelling endeavors, socio-dramatic play, and collaborative endeavors that increase social skills. The children also had access to modern technology, including laptops, light tables, cameras, phones, and overhead projectors. They were constantly inspired to explore and find innovative ways to incorporate these tools into their play, fostering a sense of creativity and adaptability.

"First I Have to Play It"

One day, Liana was playing with forest animals and wooden pieces to create the setting for her story, which she called "Forest Family." When asked about the plot, she quickly replied, "First, I have to play it; then I see what my story is." This is a paramount moment where children use materials to think about their stories. Children live in a three-dimensional world, and they need to touch, feel, manipulate, and set up a story before they can tell it in detail. As they narrate stories in their play, the plot becomes more complex, and the details grow. Their language becomes more sophisticated and their descriptions more detailed. They recognize their role as narrators and story makers.

"Forest Family."

Parallel Journey

Liana's comments piqued the educator's and Cindy's curiosity, and they were eager to explore the idea of playing a story. They embarked on this journey by researching and reading *StoryMaking: The Maker Movement Approach to Literacy for Early Learners* by Michelle Compton and Robin Thompson (2018).

Our adaptation of the story-making cycle, as discussed in the book, has evolved into a framework with the potential to significantly affect early literacy. This framework consists of distinct phases: imagine, play, make, and share. To strengthen the children's understanding of storytelling, we sought out meaningful books to help them identify key story elements, such as characters, settings, and major events. My search led me to *One Day, The End: Short, Very Short, Shorter-Than-Ever Stories* by Rebecca Kai Dotlich (2021), which quickly became a favorite among the children, because the stories were missing the "middle part." As we read, a child would say, "Hey, I have a good idea. What would happen if . . . ," which led to children sharing different scenarios and laughing as they filled in the missing parts.

The educator also followed the kindergarten standards by offering opportunities for dramatic play. When kindergarten-age children engage in complex socio-dramatic play, they act out specific roles, interact with one another in those roles, and plan how the play will go. The schedule and classroom design incorporate ample time and spaces to facilitate play.

During a group gathering, we read Liana's quote, "First, I have to play it; then I see what my story is." The educator asked the children what they thought the quote meant. Adam responded, "When you play, you can change your story." Avery added, "Building with blocks or people helps me get more ideas." According to the children's responses, together we set invitations with unscripted materials to play the story before they told the story, as Liana suggested. After playing and revisiting with the ideas from *One Day, The End*, the children recognized that each story has a beginning, middle, and end. They began to plan their stories to ensure they contained the three components, and they asked questions and reminded one another to start at the beginning and add more. This practice became standard in the children's story making.

A few days later, the educator asked the children, "What materials will you use to tell your story?" Liana would use the materials to play the story of forest animals and revisit the beginning, middle, and end of the story she was telling. She thought critically about her own storytelling techniques as she said, "I have to add more to the middle of my story." The materials fascinated her as she continued to elaborate on the details of her story. Her thought process became more intentional. Inspired

Intentionally curated materials enhance storytelling as we ask, "How might you use these materials to tell a story?"

by Liana, the other children became excited about playing, telling, and writing or sketching their unique stories. Each story demonstrated the children's ideas and theories, giving them an exciting plot that led to multiple explorations. Their sketches and simple writing served as prompts that guided their stories. This process of planning and selecting Loose Parts collections as props added a meaningful component to their literacy experiences.

The King Needs a Castle and a Boat

As the children continued to tell their stories, a spontaneous collaboration emerged. JD said, "I am building a castle for a king." Bennett suggested, "I can be the main character, the king that needs a boat." They agreed that JD would continue to build the castle while Bennett would focus on building the boat. As JD and Bennett continued to add ideas to their story, they decided to work on designing costumes they would wear to represent their characters. Bennett asked, "Miss Cindy, can we get some gold ribbons and yarn to make the crown and the long stick the king holds?" To enhance their vocabulary, I responded, "Let's research together to find out what the long stick is called." Using a tablet, we looked for the correct vocabulary term. We learned that the stick kings carry is called a scepter.

As part of the revisiting journey, the children made plans to continue their storytelling the following day. "I want to make sure we remember how I built the castle," said JD as he used a tablet to photograph his structure. While looking at the image I displayed on the smartboard, the children discussed what else they might need to continue the story. "We will know how to rebuild the castle and then we can make the crown, the scepter, and the throne." Revisiting the photo of the castle and boat block structures provided another layer to storytelling as the children chronicled their story-making process.

Parallel Journey

Through our notes and observations, we noticed that new opportunities for storytelling began to emerge. Liana continued to retell her forest animals story. JD and Bennett elaborated on their boat story. Other children showed an interest in designing a toy factory. As these multiple stories developed, we had to stay ahead of the children and be prepared to support them. We searched for meaningful books to introduce engaging invitations that included various engineering and creative challenges, as well as books that told meaningful stories. Each child had their own interests, and my role was to guide and support them through their individual and collaborative journeys. We also organized my notes and photographs by story, which allowed me to stay on top of the different pivoting points in which children rethink, reflect, redesign, and retell their stories.

Other children in the classroom engaged more in the making phase. Otto, Avery, and McKenzie began articulating that some of the creations looked like toys. This realization sparked more questions about how toys are designed. Based on their observations and discussions, they decided to transform our dramatic play area into a toy factory.

JD photographed his castle.

Parallel Journey

Rather than directing specific activities, we focused on setting up the environment with engaging invitations to observe how children construct their knowledge. My primary goal was to ensure that invitations were unscripted and focused on the process while giving children control over the final product. We selected the book *Boxitects* by Kim Smith (2020) because it tells the story of how children use their creativity to design unexpected houses, toys, and objects using unscripted materials. I thought the book would inspire the children to see themselves as learners and creators.

Reading *Boxitects* provided the children the autonomy to decide how they would relate to the story and apply what they learned. Together we formulated a question: "If you were a boxitect, how would you collaborate to design and prototype a toy?" The children applied this question to their individual stories.

Shopping list.

Otto, Avery, and McKenzie had ideas for creating toys such as airplanes, stuffed animals, and dinosaurs. The children reimagined, played, designed, redesigned, and revisited their ideas. They discussed and shared their ideas about how the story should unfold. They sketched their ideas and designs, chose materials, and ultimately decided they needed to open a toy factory.

For Bennett, the journey continued as he began to construct a boat for the king. After several days, while painting cardboard pieces, Bennett smiled and said, "Ms. Cindy, I've been working on my boat since we read *Boxitects*." His evolving story, particularly his interest in tools and boats, prompted me to review the daily anecdotes. This review underscored how Bennett entered into inquiry through technological exploration and used this inquiry process to enhance his stories.

Parallel Journey

The recent acceleration of technology demands that educators integrate meaningful and appropriate technology in early childhood classrooms. Educators can facilitate children's exploration of these technology tools to develop twenty-first-century skills such as creativity, collaboration, communication, and critical thinking.

Technology is changing how children learn, and we should capitalize on this transformation as early as possible. Children are innately curious; their curiosity drives their learning and dictates how we set up the learning environment to nurture it. The New Jersey Core Curriculum Content Standards for kindergarten require designing rich experiences that promote higher-level thinking skills while stimulating curiosity, experimentation, brainstorming, and problem solving. Play serves as the driving force for learning.

The children gathered to refine the design process of the king's boat that Bennett had started. They sketched, then selected the materials and tools they needed to build the boat.

Bennett: "Every boat needs a steering wheel. I'm going to put it in the middle."

Otto: "The wheel is not in the middle. It has to be in front. It has to connect to something to make the boat turn. I want the boat to fit more than three people."

JD: "How are you going to make it move?"

Bennett: "I don't know, but I will see if I have any screws in my house."

Bennett: "I want to have more than one boat. The smaller boat will be my delivery boat. I'm going to build a port. Sometimes people need to deliver things, and the road ends, so they put it on a big ship. The bigger boat will be for passengers."

Avery: "We will need to add a restaurant. People will have to eat when they wait."

The children created a model of a port using blocks as vessels that carried passengers to eat at the restaurant and purchase goods, deepening their math concepts as they measured and created blueprints.

Opening the toy factory.

Selecting boxes to construct a boat.

Parallel Journey

My role as a facilitator is to promote thinking through inquiry questions (cognitive development standards). I emphasize the importance of collaboration among young children. I am an active listener as children engage in individual or group work, so I can intentionally plan subsequent activities, select relevant books, and curate unscripted materials that will help children expand their knowledge. As the children continued to construct the king's boat, I framed additional questions and challenges to explore new concepts:

- What do you imagine the king will do with the boat?
- What special features does the boat have?
- How might the boat move in the water?
- What will make the boat float?

When I heard the children talking about adding a steering wheel using screws, I wondered what my next steps should be. Since many children were interested in trucks, cars, and airplanes, exploring how screws hold things together and how wheels work would be beneficial. I researched various books and decided to introduce the book *Galimoto* by Karen Lynn Williams (1990), a story about a child using metal scraps to create toys. The book also fits with my work to create a culturally responsive classroom by introducing literary characters with diverse perspectives and experiences, fostering empathy and an appreciation for ingenuity. After we read the book, the children demonstrated their resourcefulness and adaptability by using wire and other unscripted materials to design and create their own galimotos at the toy factory.

As I reviewed the children's story-making journeys, I noticed that the children had started pivoting and making connections to their everyday life interests. I realized that I needed to facilitate the transition, so I researched how I could introduce a new invitation that would inspire them to solve a new problem. As an educator, I believe that all learning experiences must be connected to children's interests. Still, it can be challenging to select books, materials, and invitations that will address all children's various and unique needs. After closely examining my notes, I outlined additional questions for the children to deepen their understanding of scientific concepts:

Investigating how wheels and axles work to construct a steering wheel.

- Bennett: "How could workers load materials onto the boat?"
- JD: "How will passengers get inside the boat?"
- Otto, Avery, and McKenzie: "How will toys be packaged and sold once they are made?"
- Liana: "Where do forest animals hibernate in the winter?"

Once the castle was built, JD's interest shifted, and he collaborated with Bennett to design the unique features of the king's boat. They discussed the motor, steering wheel, flagpole, anchor, and fishing pole. They emphasized the importance of life vests for passengers. They designed life vests to fit each child.

Our discussion on life vest safety led us to introduce and explore the concept of buoyancy. After we read *Papa's Mechanical Fish* by Candace Fleming (2013) together, the children's learning process was set in motion as they wondered how boats float and why some are designed to submerge. The rest of the children were captured by

Children construct a port with the passenger terminal.

Exploring how to load cargo.

Children chronicle their stories.

Testing buoyancy.

the discussion and the books read and shifted their interest to join JD and Bennett to build the boat. The children's learning process was not just a series of experiments but a journey that led them to test their hypotheses with various materials and make adjustments to prevent the boat from tipping over.

While playing with various unscripted materials, the children recalled the book *Susan Laughs* by Jeanne Willis (2000). This story about a girl who uses a wheelchair resonated with them for many days. I had also noticed that the children kept building ramps in the block center so people using wheelchairs could get into the king's boat.

The children began pushing the boat on the carpet, and Liana said, "We need the passengers to get in," laughing that the ship was too high. Bennett replied that they needed to build a ramp, reminding them about Susan. As a result, the children constructed a dock that was accessible to people who use wheelchairs or walkers.

At the end of the school year, we revisited Liana's quote, "I have to play it; then I see what my story is." I realized that throughout the year, the children made meaning of their words by building upon their initial story as they played. They developed attention to detail as they took ownership of their stories and created narratives with a beginning, middle, and end. They used descriptive words to visually convey their thoughts and ideas as their stories unfolded. With three-dimensional props and unscripted materials, a world of possibilities opened up, giving the children a natural way to develop their stories and express their ideas. By playing their stories, the children were able to name them.

Parallel Journey

The year concluded with the children sharing their stories. Their creativity and inquisitiveness, which I learned from and stayed engaged with, were key to our learning process. We also built trusting relationships and learned to work collaboratively. I'm confident that the children have the knowledge, skills, and disposition they need for their future school careers. It's been a rewarding year!

Building a ramp to help passengers board the vessel.

Reflective Questions

- What strategies can you design to give children the opportunity to "play their stories"?
- How will you identify your state's required educational outcomes in children's play and story making?
- What resources do you need to support children's story making?
- What knowledge do you need to increase your ability to support children's story making?
- How will you design the environment to support children's story making while meeting required outcomes?

CONCLUSION

Jessie and Miriam's Revisiting Journeys

Writing this book has been a journey of continuous reflection and growth. Each time a new theory was introduced—whether by children or fellow educators—we took the opportunity to pause, reflect, redesign, and enhance our previous insights. This collaborative process enriched our understanding and strengthened our writing. As we crafted this book, we consistently revisited our thoughts and knowledge, updating our previous work in light of new ideas.

The framework of revisiting journeys guided our thinking and deepened our understanding of our purpose as educators and as human beings. Throughout the writing process, we were challenged to humble ourselves and recognize the value of diverse perspectives. We learned to listen intently and to set aside our assumptions and expectations. This practice broadened our horizons and enriched our work, making us more open-minded and appreciative of different viewpoints. We came to believe that the time spent reflecting and redesigning our writing required us to be courageous and explore multiple avenues of thought. Some paths made us uncomfortable as they questioned our initial premises, while others validated our thinking.

Collaborating on the writing was essential to our revisiting journeys. We learned to value each other's insights, enhancing our ability to communicate our ideas. We realized that it is through effective communication that our ideas truly come to life. As we read the stories shared by other educators, we embarked on a parallel journey, pausing to question our understanding. We recognized the importance of these parallel journeys in our teaching practices, making our learning visible in ways that allowed us to change and grow. By chronicling the story of our writing, we became aware of the gaps in our narrative. We drafted multiple revisions before arriving at the final manuscript. Throughout this process, we reflected, redesigned, and continued to learn. Each step told the story of our collective and individual journeys of discovery.

Chronicling our learning story is a celebration of our accomplishments, collaboration, and the continuous growth we experience as a community of learners. It's a source of inspiration, reminding us that there's always more to learn and explore in our professional journey.

We hope this book serves as a guide and inspiration for you as you follow children's revisiting journeys.

We invite you to use the framework of the revisiting journey to guide your professional growth, enhance your teaching practices, revisit your values, and create a culture of inquiry.

—Miriam and Jessie

References

Albers, Josef. 2009. *Homage to the Square: Josef Albers.* Editorial RM.

———. 2013. *Interaction of Color.* Yale University Press.

Banko, William, Marshall L. Grant, Michael E. Jabot, Alan J. McCormack, and Thomas O'Brien. 2013. *Science for the Next Generation: Preparing for the New Standards.* https://static.nsta.org/pdfs/samples/PB336Xweb.pdf.

Brown, Stuart, and Christopher Vaughan. 2009. *Play: How It Shapes the Brain, Opens the Imagination, and Invigorates the Soul.* Avery.

Cimpian, Andrei, Lin Bian, and Sarah-Jane Leslie. 2017. "Gender Stereotypes About Intellectual Ability Emerge Early and Influence Children's Interests." *Science* 355 (6323): 389–91.

Compton, Michelle, and Robin Thompson. 2018. *StoryMaking: The Maker Movement Approach to Literacy for Early Learners.* Redleaf Press.

Csikszentmihalyi, Mihaly. 1997. *Finding Flow: The Psychology of Engagement with Everyday Life.* Basic Books.

Dewey, John. 1938. *Experience and Education.* Macmillan.

Dotlich, Rebecca Kai. 2021. *One Day, The End: Short, Very Short, Shorter-Than-Ever Stories.* Boyds Mills Press.

Fleming, Candace. 2013. *Papa's Mechanical Fish.* Farrar, Straus and Giroux.

Fromm, Erich. 1964. *The Heart of Man: Its Genius for Good and Evil.* Harper & Row.

Gross, Akeia. 2024. "Woke Wonderings." Woke Kindergarten. Accessed July 19. https://www.wokekindergarten.org/.

Holt, John. 2017. *How Children Learn.* Da Capo Press.

Kellogg, Rhoda. 1969. *Analyzing Children's Art.* Mayfield Publishing Company.

Logan, Jason. 2018. *Make Ink: A Forager's Guide to Natural Inkmaking.* Abrams.

Maher, Alison, and Andrea Sisbarro. 2018. "A Contextual Approach to Planning: Developing a Curriculum That Engages Both Children and Adults." Presentation at Boulder Journey School Summer Conference, Boulder, CO, June 21.

Malaguzzi, Loris. 1993. "For an Education Based on Relationships." Translated by Lella Gandini. *Young Children* 49 (1): 9–12.

Malaguzzi, Loris, and C. Musatti. 1996. "L'Importanza di Rivedersi / The Importance of Seeing Yourself Again." In *I cento linguaggi dei bambini: Narrativa del possibile/The Hundred Languages of Children: Narrative of the Possible*, ed. T. Filippini and V. Vecchi, 46–52. Reggio Children.

Marron, Dylan. 2018. "Empathy Is Not Endorsement." TED Talk, April. www.ted.com/talks/dylan_marron_empathy_is_not_endorsement.

Pelo, Ann. 2017. *The Language of Art: Inquiry-Based Studio Practices in Early Childhood Settings.* Redleaf Press.

Rinaldi, Carlina. 2011. "The Pedagogy of Listening: The Listening Perspective from Reggio Emilia." *Innovations* 8 (4): 1–4.

Russo, Marisabina. 2015. *Little Bird Takes a Bath.* Schwartz & Wade Books.

Siegel, Daniel J. 2023. *IntraConnected: MWe (Me + We) as the Integration of Self, Identity, and Belonging*. W. W. Norton & Company.

Smith, Kim. 2020. *Boxitects*. Clarion Books.

Solórzano, Daniel G., and Tara J. Yosso. 2002. "Critical Race Methodology: Counter-Storytelling as an Analytical Framework for Education Research." *Qualitative Inquiry* 8(1): 23-44. https://doi.org/10.1177/107780040200800103.

Vygotsky, Lev S., Michael Cole, Sally Stein, and Allan Sekula. 1978. *Mind in Society: The Development of Higher Psychological Processes*. Harvard University Press.

Williams, Karen Lynn. 1990. *Galimoto*. Lothrop, Lee & Shepard Books.

Willis, Jeanne. 2000. *Susan Laughs*. Henry Holt.

Wilson, Edward O. 1984. *Biophilia: The Human Bond with Other Species*. Harvard University Press.

Index

action research, 48, 69
activities, to elicit compliance, 1
adaptability, developing, 2
adult play, described, 48–49
Albers, Annie, 72
Albers, Josef, 72
Alice's Adventures in Wonderland (Carroll), 8
analysis, learning through revisiting journeys, 30
  See also ecosystem, journey into local
art and making meaning of thinking, 31
assessments, reflecting on, 63
Atkins, Jeannine, 187
audio recordings, in observations, 39

being and becoming, children exploring identities and, 24
belonging
  importance of, 141
  learning and, 27
  play ecosystems and, 36
binders for children, 58–60, 63
biophilia, 32, 189
  See also birds, journey with
birds, journey with
  children's actions, 172–180, 181, 182–185, 186–187, 188–189
  length of, 171
  parallel journey of educators, 173, 174, 175, 180–182, 186, 188, 189
  reflecting on, 189
books, approaches to reading, 2
Boulder Journey School (Boulder, Colorado), 153–169
Boxitects (Smith), 198
Brown, Stuart, 22
Brunt, James, 117, 118

Carroll, Lewis, 8
Center of Gravity preschool (California), 29
children's journeys
  birds journey, 172–180, 181, 182–185, 186–187, 188–189
  color theory journey, 71–72, 73, 74–76, 77–78, 80–84
  ecosystem journey, 124, 125–130, 132–134, 135–137
  fire into shelter journey, 154, 155–156, 157–158, 159–160, 161–162, 163–167
  identity journey through stitching stories, 143, 144, 145–146, 147, 148, 149–151
  making natural ink journey, 90–91, 93–94, 95–97, 99–100, 101, 102–103
  spinners (spirals) and mandalas journey, 106, 108–109, 111, 112–113, 114–117, 118–121
  story making journey, 192, 193–194, 195–197, 198, 199, 201–202
chronicles/chronicling
  accessibility of, 59, 60
  assessing planning through, 14
  at beginning of year, 55
  as collaboration, 56, 116
  described, 14, 55
  guidelines for
    account for recording and supervision, 56–57, 58
    methods, 56, 58–60
    reflecting with children, 57
    tools for, 57
  importance of, 55
  incorporating families into, 62
  ink making journey, 101–102
  local ecosystem journey, 124–125, 131–132
  meeting state-required outcomes with, 192
  parallel journeys of educators, 49
  reflecting on, 57–58, 60, 121
  of revisiting journeys, 14
  spinners (spirals) and mandalas journey, 115, 116–117
  of story making journey, 192
  using to make educator's role visible to families, 61–63
  See also observation
chronicle walls, 56, 58, 70
classrooms. *See* play ecosystems
collaboration
  with children, 69–70, 116
  chronicling as, 56, 116
  fire into shelter journey, 154–155, 157
  identity through stitching stories, 144–145, 146–147, 148–149
  with infants, 163–167
  at Kinderoo Children's Academy, 141–142
  learning through revisiting journeys, 31
  play ecosystems as inviting, 36, 37
  reflecting with children, 57
collaboration among educators
  benefits of, 50
  chronicling and, 56
  color theory journey, 68–70, 71, 74, 76–77, 79
  communication and, 56
  fire into shelter journey, 167–169
  ink making journey, 92–93, 98, 100
  on journey into local ecosystem, 126, 128, 131
  local ecosystem journey, 135
  parallel journeys and, 50
  reflecting as team, 50–51
  spinners (spirals) and mandalas journey, 106–107, 112, 113–114, 116, 117
  time to reflect as team, 42–44
collaborative portfolios/binders, 58–60

color theory journey
children's actions, 71–72, 73, 74–76, 77–78, 80–84
collaboration among educators, 69–70, 71, 74, 76–77, 79
color wheel, 79–83
parallel journey of educators, 69, 71, 72–73, 74, 76–77, 79–80, 84–86
play ecosystems for, 70–71
reflecting on, 68, 69, 70, 71, 72–73, 74, 79–80, 87
color wheels, 79–83
communication
making educator's role visible to families, 61–63
between members of team of educators, 56
self-portraits as, 142
types of, 47
community
building, 18–19
children defining, 163—164
designing play ecosystems and, 38
group gatherings as, 38
learning as reciprocal process unfolding within, 27
partnerships with, 49, 51–52
as part of children's identities, 28
play and, 23, 27–28
premise of, 19
reflecting on, 28
See also ecosystem, journey into local
Compton, Michelle, 195
confidence, gaining, 18
counterstorytelling, 158–159
COVID, 154
See also fire into shelter journey
creativity, 16, 168
critical race theory, 158–159
critical thinking, enhancing, 18
curiosity
embracing inquiry to nurture, 17
fostering and guiding children's natural, 12
learning through revisiting journeys, 30
as lens for observing children's engagement and interactions, 42
parallel journeys of educators and, 14, 47
time needed for developing, 18

danmalas, 107, 117, 118
da Vinci, Leonardo, 144
democracy, learning through revisiting journeys, 31
Dewey, John, 48
documentation/documenting. *See* chronicles/chronicling
Dotlich, Rebecca Kai, 195

ecosystem, journey into local
children's actions, 124, 125–130, 132–134, 135–137
chronicling, 124–125, 131–132
family participation in, 128
parallel journey of educators, 124–125, 126, 128, 131–132, 133, 134–135, 137, 138–139
reflecting on, 126, 128, 135, 139, 189
ecosystems, 35
See also play ecosystems
educators
as architects of play ecosystems, 13
intentionality of, 39
learning about children from families, 68
making role visible to families, 61–63
personal experiences of, 41, 47
praxis of, 23, 25
problem solving by, 92
relationship between children and, routines and activities designed to elicit compliance and, 1
requirements for, to shift from pedagogical to heutagogical approach, 9–10
use of pivoting points by, 9
See also collaboration among educators; parallel journeys of educators
emotional literacy, developing, 146, 147
emotions and identity, 146
"Empathy Is Not Endorsement" (Marron), 158
Engel, Jacie, 167–168
ephemerality, concept of, 107
evaluation, 30
See also ecosystem, journey into local
expectations, letting go of, 107
experience and meaning making, 26
exploration, 26, 30

fairy tales and scariness, 157, 159
families
children's identities and, 146
learning about children from, 68
making educator's role visible to, 61–63
participating in journeys
inkmaking, 103
local ecosystem, 128
spinners (spirals) and mandalas, 108
feelings, play ecosystems and, 37
Ferguson, Fabian E., 144
fire into shelter journey
background of, 154
children's actions, 154, 155–156, 157–158, 159–160, 161–162, 163–167
parallel journey of educators, 154–155, 157, 158–159, 161, 162–163, 165, 167–169
reflecting on, 161, 167–168, 169
Fleming, Candace, 201
Follow the Flyway (Nelson), 179
freedom and meaning making, 26
Fromm, Erich, 32

Galimoto (Williams), 200
Gennarelli, Cindy, 191–203
goodbye, ritual of saying, 38
Gross, Akeia, 168
group gatherings as community, 38

handwritten notes of observations, 39
Hase, Stewart, 3
heutagogy
described, 3
play as learning and, 22
requirements for educators to shift from pedagogical approach to learning to, 9–10
history, learning through revisiting journeys, 30
Holt, John, 22
Homage to the Square (J. Albers), 72
How Children Learn (Holt), 22

identity/identities of children
community and, 28
importance of, 141
play and, 23, 24
providing opportunities for children to explore, 24
reflecting on, 24
identity journey through stitching stories
children's actions, 143, 144, 145–146, 147, 148, 149–151
designing play ecosystems for, 149
parallel journey of educators, 142–143, 144–145, 146–147, 148–149
reflecting on, 151
inductive reasoning, learning through revisiting journeys, 30
See also color theory journey
infants, collaborating with, 163–167
ink, making natural journey
beginning of, 89–91
children's actions, 90–91, 93–94, 95–97, 99–100, 101, 102–103
chronicling, 101–102
families participating in, 103
in medieval times, 102–103
parallel journey of educators, 91, 92–93, 94–95, 96, 97–99, 100, 101–102
reflecting on, 92–93, 98, 103
inquiry/inquiries
by children into own identities, 24
creating cultures of, 16–17
curiosity and, 12
described, 22
love of learning and, 9
nurturing curiosity by embracing, 17
parallel journeys of educators and creating culture of, 47
planning, 8, 12
play ecosystems and, 13
intentionality of educators, 39
Interaction of Color (J. Albers), 72
interpretation, learning through revisiting journeys, 31
In the Mirror (Ferguson), 144
IntraConnected (Siegel), 165

journeys, revisiting
benefits of, 1–2, 8
building community, 18–19
creating cultures of inquiry, 16–17
developing sense of self, 18
enhancing critical thinking, 18
increasing children's learning, 15–16
learning to listen, 17
new ideas, knowledge, and perspectives, 8
searching for meaning, 17–18
chronicling, 14
educators' parallel journeys and, 14–15, 18
essence of, 17
following paths of own interest, 2
framework for, 12–15
growth in complexity through, 25
incorporating families into chronicling process and, 62
long-term, 169
making educator's role visible to families and, 61–63
meaning making and, 26
methods for
chronicle walls, 56, 58
collaborative portfolios/binders, 58–60
storyboards, 59
play ecosystems and
designing responsive, 13
as facilitating, 35, 36, 37
importance of, 49
supporting by understanding relationship between children and, 14
principles reflected by, 25
reflecting on ways to support children's, 44
researching, 28–29
supporting, using observation and reflection, 41–42
types of, 29, 30–32
See also specific journeys

Kellogg, Rhoda, 106–107
Kenyon, Chris, 3
Kinderoo Children's Academy (Ocala, Florida), 141–151
Klein, Kathy, 107, 117

Land Art: Creating Artworks in and with the Landscape (Brunt), 118
language, 31
See also story making journey
The Language of Art (Pelo), 142

learning
belonging and, 27
children's motivation for, 15
chronicling and making relevant, 49
by doing, 22, 48
as dynamic, individualized process, 2
educator's, to guide children's revisiting journeys, 48
elements encompassed during meaning making, 26
elements of long-lasting, 10
inquiries and love of, 9
messiness of, as catalyst for creativity, 16
as natural for all children, 10
play as
community and, 23, 27–28
described, 22
heutagogy of, 22
identity and, 23, 24
meaning making and, 23, 26–27
praxis, 23, 25
research on, 22
valuing, 22–23
principles for designing, 24
as reciprocal process unfolding within community, 27
requirements for educators to shift from pedagogical to heutagogical approach to, 9–10
revisiting journeys increase children's, 15–16
routines and activities designed to elicit compliance and, 1
self-directed, as necessary, 2
learning spaces. *See* play ecosystems
listening, 17, 91
literacy. *See* story making journey
Little Bird Takes a Bath (Russo), 185
Logan, Jason, 98
logico-mathematical thinking, learning through revisiting journeys, 30
Loose Parts, learning when playing with, 23, 176

Make Ink: A Forager's Guide to Natural Inkmaking (Logan), 98
Malaguzzi, Loris, 142, 163
mandalas
emergence of designs, 106–107
as spiritual symbols, 109, 110
mark making, 154–155
Marron, Dylan, 158
materials
educator's exploration of, offered to children, 48–49
identifying children's journeys and, 13
unscripted, 23, 176
McLerran, Alice, 7

meaning, making
described, 26
language and, 31
learning elements encompassed during, 26
play and, 23
reflecting on, 26
story making journey and, 191–192
meaning, revisiting journey as quest for, 17
metacognition, learning through revisiting journeys, 30
mindflex attitude, 98
mistakes, as opportunities, 8, 37
Munsch, Robert, 157
My Modern Met (website), 117

nature, 32, 189
See also birds, journey with
negotiation, learning through revisiting journeys, 31
Nelson, Sarah, 179

observation(s)
curiosity as lens for, 42
designing responsive play ecosystems and, 39
need for "quiet mind" for, 42
notes on, 39–40
photos in, 39, 40
selecting time for, 56
using, in designing responsive play ecosystems, 41
using, when supporting revisiting journeys, 41–42
One Day, The End: Short, Very Short, Shorter-Than-Ever Stories (Dotlich), 195

paint making with flowers exploration, 97–99
Papa's Mechanical Fish (Fleming), 201
The Paper Bag Princess (Munsch), 157
parallel journeys of educators
as action research, 48, 69
actions of, 68
birds' journey, 173, 174, 175, 180–182, 186, 188, 189
color theory journey, 69, 71, 72–73, 74, 76–77, 79–80, 84–86
developing, 14–15
fire into shelter journey, 154–155, 157, 158–159, 161, 162–163, 165, 167–169
as fostering reflection, 18, 47
as helping educators, 49–50
identity through stitching stories journey, 142–143, 144–145, 146–147, 148–149
importance of, 64, 67
ink theory journey, 91, 92–93, 94–95, 96, 97–99, 100, 101–102
at Kinderoo Children's Academy, 142
local ecosystem journey, 124–125, 126, 128, 131–132, 133, 134–135, 137, 138–139
making educator's role visible to families and, 61–63

planning, 69–70
in practice, 50–52
reflecting on, 52, 62
spinners (spirals) and mandalas journey, 106–107, 109–111, 112, 113–114, 115, 116, 117
story making journey, 192–193, 195, 197, 198–199, 200–201, 203
"The Pedagogy of Listening: The Listening Perspective from Reggio Emilia" (Rinaldi), 17, 155
Pelo, Ann, 142
photos, in observations, 39, 40
physicality, learning through revisiting journeys, 31
pivoting points, 9, 11
play
designing responsive ecosystems for, 13
as learning
community and, 23, 27–28
described, 22
heutagogy of, 22
identity and, 23, 24
meaning making and, 23, 26–27
praxis, 23, 25
research on, 22
valuing, 22–23
observing, 13
relationships between children and adults and, 18–19
symbolic, 30
Play: How It Shapes the Brain, Opens the Imagination, and Invigorates the Soul (Brown and Vaughan), 22
play ecosystems
benefits of well-designed, 35–36
for color theory journey, 70–71
components of
physical space, 36–37
socio-emotional space, 37
temporal space, 37–38
designing, 68
for children to visit portfolios, 60
for identity journey through stitching stories, 149
responsive, 13, 38–41, 51
using observation in, 41
diverse voices in, 2
elements of democratic, 10
explorations of identities and, 24
as inviting collaboration, 36, 37
meaning making in action and, 27
praxis by children in action and, 25
reflecting on, 41, 44, 203
revisiting journeys and, 49
understanding relationship between children and, to support journeys, 14
portfolios, 58–60, 63
power, learning, 31
See also fire into shelter journey
praxis
described, 25
play and, 23
reflecting on, 25
problem solving, 26, 92

radical empathy, developing, 158, 159, 169
rangoli, 108
reasoning, inductive, 30
reflection/reflections
on assessments, 63
on birds' journey, 189
on children's identities, 24
on children's portfolios, 63
on chronicling, 57–58, 60
on color theory journey, 68, 69, 70, 71, 72–73, 74, 79–80, 87
on community, 28
on fire into shelter journey, 161, 167–168, 169
on identity journey, 151
importance of, 39
on ink making theory journey, 92–93, 98, 103
at Kinderoo Children's Academy, 141–142
on local ecosystem journey, 126, 128, 135, 139, 189
on making educator's role visible to families, 62
on meaning making, 26
on parallel journeys of educators, 18, 47, 52, 62
on play ecosystems, 41, 44, 203
on praxis, 25
on spinners (spirals) and mandalas journey, 121
on story making journey, 203
as team of educators, 50–51
time for educators to practice, 42–44
using observation when supporting revisiting journeys, 41–42
on using technology, 151
on ways to support children's revisiting journeys, 44
relationships between children and adults, play as inspiring, 18–19
replication, learning through revisiting journeys, 30
See also identity journey through stitching stories; spinners (spirals) and mandalas journey
resilience, developing, 2
Rinaldi, Carlina, 17, 155
Robin's Home (Atkins), 187
routines, designed to elicit compliance, 1
Roxaboxen (McLerran), 7
Russo, Marisabina, 185

scariness, investigating. *See* fire into shelter journey
science, development of rudimentary understanding of concepts across content areas of, 9
scientific thinking, learning, 30
See also ecosystem, journey into local; ink, making natural journey

self, sense of, developing, 18
self-directed learning, as necessary, 2
self-portraits, 142
self-talk, 31
Siegel, Daniel J., 165
skin color exploration, 143
Smith, Kim, 198
Solórzano, Daniel G., 158–159
spiders, investigating, 156–157
spinners (spirals) and mandalas journey
  children's actions, 106, 108–109, 111, 112–113, 114–117, 118–121
  chronicling, 115, 116–117
  families participating in, 108
  parallel journey of educators, 106–107, 109–111, 112, 113–114, 115, 116, 117
  reflecting on, 121
state standards and required outcomes, 192, 193, 195, 199, 203
storyboards, 59
story making, learning through, 31
  See also story making journey
StoryMaking: The Maker Movement Approach to Literacy for Early Learners (Compton and Thompson), 195
story making journey
  children's actions, 192, 193–194, 195–197, 198, 199, 201–202
  making meaning and, 191–192
  parallel journey of educators, 192–193, 195, 197, 198–199, 200–201, 203
  reflecting on, 203
Susan Laughs (Willis), 202
symbolic play, 30
symmetry exploration, 144–146

tactile media, 148–151
teachable moments, described, 9
technology
  learning through exploration of, 30
  using, 144–145, 151, 161, 198–199
thinking, learning through revisiting journeys, 30
Thompson, Robin, 195
transformation, children exploring identities and, 24

Vaughan, Christopher, 22
videos, in observations, 39, 40, 57
The Vitruvian Man, (da Vinci), 144
Vygotsky, Lev, 31

water absorption exploration, 94–97
William Paterson University Child Development Center, 171–189, 191–203
Williams, Karen Lynn, 200
Willis, Jeanne, 202
Wilson, Edward O., 32
woodworking, 181–183

Yosso, Tara J., 158–159

Zimbelman, Kirsten, 153